GOLD STANDARD

How to Rock the World and Run an Empire

KYM GOLD

CO-CREATOR OF
TRUE RELIGION BRAND JEANS

WITH
SHARON SOBOIL

T0306916

Skyhorse Publishing

Copyright © 2015 by Kym Gold
First paperback edition © 2021 by Kym Gold

All rights reserved. No part of this book may be reproduced in any manner without the express written consent of the publisher, except in the case of brief excerpts in critical reviews or articles. All inquiries should be addressed to Skyhorse Publishing, 307 West 36th Street, 11th Floor, New York, NY 10018.

Skyhorse Publishing books may be purchased in bulk at special discounts for sales promotion, corporate gifts, fund-raising, or educational purposes. Special editions can also be created to specifications. For details, contact the Special Sales Department, Skyhorse Publishing, 307 West 36th Street, 11th Floor, New York, NY 10018 or info@skyhorsepublishing.com.

Skyhorse® and Skyhorse Publishing® are registered trademarks of Skyhorse Publishing, Inc.®, a Delaware corporation.

Visit our website at www.skyhorsepublishing.com.

10 9 8 7 6 5 4 3 2 1

Library of Congress Cataloging-in-Publication Data is available on file.

Cover design by Laura Klynstra
Cover photo credit: Russell Baer

ISBN: 978-1-5107-6586-3
Ebook ISBN: 978-1-5107-0151-9

Printed in the United States of America

I want to dedicate this book to my mom, Nikki.
Without her, I wouldn't be me.

CONTENTS

INTRODUCTION

Today, with so many women becoming responsible for being the breadwinner in the family, it is even more imperative that there be equality between the sexes in business. And yet, speaking as a woman, we're not there yet. As the only woman on a board of directors of an IPO (Initial Public Offering) company I helped to create, this fact has been made crystal clear to me.

My intent with this book is to provide insights into what happened to me in my life that could be useful to other women who either want to create a company and take it public or shatter the proverbial glass ceiling. This story is also for those of you who need a little inspiration from a woman rather than a man in the upper echelon of my industry, the fashion business.

I share the raw and honest truths of what my world has been like, from struggles to find my own individuality having been born a triplet, to what it is to build an international brand, to the thrill and defeat of creating and then losing companies. In this book, I share how that looked as a mother and a wife, a balance struggle that many women endure.

There are invaluable lessons I learned in being inducted into the richest one percent of Americans. It took a lot of hard work and heartbreak. People may think that money fixes everything. It does not. In fact, having money adds another layer in life to manage, something I continue to learn how to maneuver through on a daily basis.

I am a creative artist and I love what I do. So when people ask me why I still work, my answer has always been, "Why wouldn't I? Does a painter stop painting?"

To create is to live, and I have so much more living to do—especially as I keep rediscovering what I can contribute as a woman in this man-centric business and in life. If I can pass on the wisdom I've accumulated to make it easier or better for the next army of talented, passionate women, then I've done my job.

One

THE FABRIC

It has been said who you are today has everything to do with your childhood. I knew, for me, that this theory was relevant. Throughout my life I had fiercely searched to find my own voice, to stand out and not be dismissed, and to take credit when due. Those were themes that ran through my life as one of an identical three.

When I was born, doctors didn't have ultrasound yet, so my unsuspecting mom didn't know she was pregnant with three girls. Identical triplets. She had already had my brother Scott.

She found out seven months in, when they did an x-ray. She was busy with getting her dress back over her engorged belly when the doctor returned with her x-ray in hand.

"*What*?!" she and my dad cried in disbelief.

Two weeks later, we were fighting to get out. We were seven weeks early. Doctors had found that the later you are in the birthing order, the less air you have to breathe before being delivered. This caused concern at the possibility of brain damage for the later siblings, so they only did

C-sections for multiple births after us. I was the last one out. Imagine that.

When no one expects triplets, you come out of your mom's belly and enter the world as a burden. The idea of having an instant family of six (in our case), when they thought it was going to be a manageable family of four, is a lot for a parent to wrap her head around. The cute outfit they bought for the one bundle of joy needs to be tripled. The time. The energy. The attention. All tripled. It becomes a completely different conversation . . . in triplicate.

My mom and dad had spent considerable time deciding on the name of their soon-to-be-born baby. In a moment's notice, they were expected to come up with two more first and middle names. We were given the names Michelle Lynn, Traci Lee, and Kymberly Jill.

There was a study done in 1983 that showed a mother of six-month-old triplets expended approximately 197 hours per week on care for those babies, when there are actually only 168 hours in week. Clearly they had help, but it still wasn't easy.

It could have been worse. We were quadruplets originally, but my mom miscarried a month before our birth, making us triplets in the end. Monozygotic triplets, which means we were identical from the result of a single egg splitting after conception. We were literally one in a million.

Michelle and Traci were born mirrored, meaning that their hair falls in opposite directions to each other and their fingerprints are mirrored, with one being right-handed while the other left-handed. I was probably a mirror too, with the fourth baby that was miscarried.

The moment we greedily sucked up our first breath of air in the world, the three of us were immediately separated and thrust inside incubators. We spent most of our first seven weeks of life in a plastic dome, with tubes and wires protruding from our impossibly small bodies, barely having entered this world of challenges.

I can only imagine how it must have felt when my mom and dad saw our tiny bodies reach for the nurses instead of them. They watched helplessly and hoped their new beautiful babies would survive.

We were each born six minutes apart.

My theory is that the last one out is the eldest, because you are the first one conceived. If you are the first conceived, then you are the one furthest in the back.

And truly, I have always felt as though I am the oldest. I am the one who did everything first—the first to have kids, get married, and start a career.

My parents went from one to suddenly four kids in a matter of eighteen minutes. Who wants four kids under the age of two all at once? Well, as it turned out, my father didn't. He left my mom a year later, after having had an affair with another woman. Traci, Michelle, and I were one-year-olds, and my brother was two-and-a-half.

Our parents were not happy in their marriage. There was a time before the divorce when our mom showed up at dad's office in her robe. She paraded us through his law office, past the partners, secretaries, and associates, and plunked us before dad, saying, "Here! They're yours too." And she marched out.

After dad left, mom became very depressed, as not only did he leave her with the four babies, but she discovered her father was dying, too. It was bad timing, and her sorrow was palpable. It was impossibly painful to see my mom, a very strong, bright woman, with a great quirky style, who was a loving mother, devastated by a sense of loss from not one, but two men at the same time.

In our little kid minds, we believed we made our dad leave. We felt as though we were the cause of our mom's suffering. And later, in finding out there was another woman involved, it initiated in me the deep-rooted fear that men can't be trusted or depended on.

I can only imagine my mother's sense of helplessness at the situation in which she found herself. She couldn't work with four babies to tend to and had to rely on my dad for child support, which was never enough. She had full custody, and he would take us on Wednesdays and every other weekend. Hardly a respite for her.

Under the best of circumstances, we were a handful. My mom used to sew on our pajamas because we always took them off at night. Michelle would climb out of her crib, take her pajamas off, and crawl out a window in our bedroom. When she came back inside, she would be covered with soot from the barbecue, asking, "What?" She was always more adventurous. I would much rather sleep. Given the option of any activity, I would gladly choose a nap.

As our parents were going through their nasty divorce, we were traveling between the two of them. Even though I had my siblings, I just couldn't shake the feeling of tremendous sadness. We were all having a hard time with the divorce. We became the perfect ongoing conduit for our parents' anger. My dad married Sherry, the woman he had left my mom for. She had two sons of her own. Craig and Kevin were a few years older than us. And now Sherry had my dad; they were his family now. The last thing Sherry wanted was the Goldman entourage in the mix. At least that's how it felt.

When we were four years old, my mom met my stepdad, George, on a blind date. He was a lawyer like my dad. In fact, both men had gone to Berkeley and were personal injury attorneys; George's last name is Goldberg, and my dad's Goldman. She didn't even need to change her hand towels.

I always joked, "That's a law firm right there."

We all loved George. He sat my sisters, brother, and I down and asked us if he could marry our mom. We were putty in his hands and felt proud he had included us in the conversation. Mom was happy again, that was most important to us.

George had an entrepreneurial spirit, with a bit of danger mixed in, which made him incredibly charismatic and someone I would emulate in later years. Marrying George allowed our mom to focus on being a wife and raising us. We, too, were now a family.

We all resided in the San Fernando Valley, California. The home of "the Valley Girl speak." Thankfully I had left before starting to talk like one. Michelle, Traci, Scott, and I lived with mom and George in Tarzana. Sherry and our dad lived in Studio City with Sherry's two boys. For me, it would later become an agonizing ride straight down the 101 freeway.

One thing my sisters and I agreed on was how much we did not like our new stepmother. It bonded us, and we stuck together for salvation. We'd come to each other's defense and rescue no matter what. Of course, later, as an adult looking back, I realized most children don't like their stepparents, certainly not in the beginning, and we were no different.

Sherry was not fond of us either. When talking to my dad, Sherry would chide, "They sound like chickens." If one triplet was told to be quiet, all of us were expected to adhere. She treated us like drones. My brother Scott got the worst of it. As much as I felt a dismissal from my dad and Sherry, as a boy, Scott was lost in the mix. We girls had each other. We were lethal, even when Sherry would stick up for her sons in an argument. But, when we reprimanded her boys for hitting our older brother, she would come down on Scott like a lioness protecting her cub. It was only in later years that I would be able to empathize with her; at the time it was all very heightened.

Scott never got much attention. He had really bad asthma, so he couldn't do sports, while my stepbrothers were star athletes. On Sundays, when we would wait for mom, Scott's asthma would get so bad that Sherry would put him in the other room to sit by himself because his breathing, as she would put it, was "affecting everybody else." Sadly, Scott's need to defend himself so often is something I think he has never gotten over.

Sherry would talk horribly about my mom, too. Although in fairness, my mom had nothing good to say about Sherry either. Any physical attributes we got from my mom, Sherry would comment on. She often called us "ragamuffins," because our clothes were muddy when they picked us up. Although she knew full well that we had just been playing, she would comment how dirty we looked. She'd even call us fat, which was ludicrous because we had been born weighing three pounds each! We were so skinny. I attribute my weight issues as an adult to her insensitive comments.

During those formative years, I never felt complete because I was always getting just a third of everything: a third of attention, food, clothes, love, energy, etc. Whatever it was, it was a third of the whole. We were clumped together as "the girls," not individuals, but "one."

My dad was oblivious. It was a free-for-all at his house. There were so many kids that we were never supervised. We would constantly get blistered from the sun, and I continually got hurt. My dad had no time for us. He had other issues when it was time to teach us to tie our shoes or ride a bike.

It was the antithesis at my mom's. George gave us a sense of belonging. He loved us and gave us attention. We would go on great vacations together, and I remember how thrilled he was to take off our training wheels and to teach us how to pedal and steer our bikes—something that was such a bother to my dad.

We had several dogs, a long-haired German Shepherd named Kasha, a Great Dane named Sultan, and a Shar-pei named Meeskait, which means "little ugly one" in Yiddish. George would constantly bring home abandoned dogs, and my mom would find them a new home two weeks later. It was a joyful household, and full of life.

George's mother, Grandma Sylvia, moved to LA from New York. She was a typical Jewish grandmother. I loved her, and she was everything to me. She brought a kind of ceremony to our family functions that comes from having elders present. She gave us a sense of history and a feeling of belonging to something bigger. We had Passover, Hanukkah, and semi-regular Shabbat at mom's house with Grandma Sylvia.

When I was six, my younger brother, Adam, was born. All the kids couldn't wait to get home to see him. We all loved that little boy. We would vie for time to hold him.

A month later, Sherry and my dad had a baby boy as well; they named him Sean. It made for a constant cacophony at both houses. The UnBrady Bunch, if you will.

Especially now, with the new babies, our parents would clump the triplets together. There was so much drama that was exacerbated by the three of us. We were too loud amongst the others, so instead we weren't heard at all. At my dad's, the Goldman kids were always second place to Sherry's kids. They began keeping us on the periphery. For birthdays and holidays, any kind of celebration, they sat us at a different table. It helped me to build my burgeoning argument of, "Why would I want to go over there?"

If it was not chaotic enough at my dad's house, he would take us on camping trips. He and Sherry would take all seven kids to the lake. It would always start on a positive note, as we pitched tents, made s'mores, and drank Ovaltine while telling scary stories late into the night. But it seemed to always end in a crisis, with someone getting hurt or some catastrophe happening on each trip.

The summer of '72, we got nestled into our campsite. All the kids were running around, and I wandered off the wrong way. I took a wrong turn and suddenly, I couldn't find the campsite. There was nothing I recognized, and my cries for help went unanswered. I was six years old, wandering around the forest, scared shitless, and no one had noticed I wasn't among the group. It took eight excruciating hours before I managed to take the correct turn that led me back to the campsite. I sat down amongst the others.

My dad's idea of cajoling me was saying, "We didn't even realize you were missing." He hadn't even noticed I was gone!

I was furious at him. It concerned me that a man I loved and relied on would let me down. It invited the notion that I wanted to be self-sufficient in future, and never depend on a man.

One time I rode home from San Diego to my mom's house in Tarzana, about a two-hour drive, with a broken arm. There were seven of us in the car all clamoring for attention and talking at once, so when I tried to tell them I had a problem, I was told to be quiet. When I got to my mom's, I didn't tell her or George either. However, George quickly realized I was in pain and immediately took me to the doctor.

Not long after came the final hurrah for me. We were at a function with my dad and Sherry, riding a horse. She was a beautiful chestnut with a long black mane, huge in comparison to our eight-year-old bodies. We loved to canter and got a thrill from the thrust of energy. It was much more fun than the hard pounding of a trot. Michelle and I were cantering, but didn't have a good enough hold when the horse slowed back into a trot, and we both bobbled over, hurtling off her onto the packed dirt. Michelle fell hard, directly on top of me. She was hysterical.

My dad scooped us up and drove to the nearby emergency room. I didn't want to be a burden, so I didn't say anything. When we saw a doctor, it turned out Michelle had only sprained her wrist. As if an afterthought, knowing I had fallen off the horse too, the doctor did a cursory examination of me. I was diagnosed with a broken shoulder and elbow, and had to wear a mid-body cast. The doctor took a full body x-ray to ensure I didn't have any other injuries, because I was so quiet.

After the horse accident, I rather bluntly asked mom, "Can I stop going to dad's house?" There were just too many kids and I never felt a real part of that family.

My mom understood my request. I did also want to be easier on her. This way she wouldn't have to constantly take me to the doctor for injuries acquired over there.

When I stopped visiting, my dad thought my mom put me up to it. That was not what I had wanted to happen. Now I had created a whole new issue for them to argue over. The other girls continued to go over. I thought he would be grateful to have one less kid to look after! But instead, it started yet another war. My intent to make it easier for my mom and myself had backfired completely.

In staying home, I was in heaven. I got to spend time with my mom and stepdad, with just my half-brother there. It was fantastic! In comparison, it almost felt like I was an only child! I got to sleep by myself, eat what I wanted, and watch what I preferred on TV. I didn't have to share anything! It was a completely novel existence that I loved. I didn't know of any life other than being one of three.

It was the summer going into fourth grade. I was so excited to finally be my own person and go somewhere without my sisters! I was supposed to go to Italy for three months with my best friend, Nancy Carmelli. She was a friend to all of us, but she took me! It was a fantastic time away, but I could only last two weeks. As soon as I got there, it was as though something was missing, and I needed to go home.

The dichotomy in trying to find my identity is that it had always been like a push/pull. At the time, my sisters and I all had really long hair. I was happy about coming home but when I arrived, Traci and Michelle had cut all their hair off! So I cut all my hair off, too. It was like being in the mafia. I wanted out, but they pulled me back in.

Michelle was always known as dad's favorite. She was definitely a daddy's girl. When I started staying at mom's, she stayed at dad's. Traci continued to go back and forth and tried to find ways to get dad's attention. I didn't want his attention. At any opportunity of intimacy, I would walk the other way.

It was the seventies when we were in the third and fourth grade. Short of sending us off to an ashram, our parents had us pretty much trying everything in regards to self-discovery and reflection. I'm sure we seemed troubled. We were still feeling the repercussions of their dramatic divorce.

Mom would go through various fads of removing sugar and soda from our diets. Instead, she'd make fruit smoothies infused with bee pollen and flaxseed. She also began to cook strictly vegetarian meals and to meditate often.

My stepbrothers, Craig and Kevin, were now in high school. Craig was becoming a bully. I was at a loss for what to do. I would dread being near him and didn't feel safe at my dad's.

When I went to my dad and Sherry to complain, and they'd wave me off, it was soul-crushing to have my own parent not advocate for me.

During my pre-teen years, my temper was out of control. We were signed up for meditation classes, did chanting, and the infamous Erhard Seminars Training (EST) with Werner Erhard. I can assure you I was not happy having to hold my pee for hours, waiting for a designated bathroom break, as dictated to us while in the seminar. By then I was not in the mood to be told what to do. And that, especially, was not working for me.

As I reflect back, it was a pivotal point in my "self discovery" when I realized I had an issue with what made these gurus think their perspective was the *only* way, or the right way. I didn't get it. I didn't get why Werner, Deepak, the Maharishi, all of them, were trying to control people.

We were sitting in full lotus position, listening to one guru or another spout his opinionated long-winded bullshit when I finally stood up and said, "I just want to get out of this fucking shit!" Over a hundred people turned and glared at me.

I couldn't step over the cross-legged sea of devotees quickly enough. And my sisters followed right behind me. We were done with the enlightened years.

Sometimes you need to stand your ground. If you know something doesn't feel right, heed that warning. Hopefully it will keep you safe into the future and become more refined with time. Often, when you choose a different route, or a path that is not the accepted choice of others, but feels better for you, it can cause dissension. It is the life of a leader, not a follower.

There is no need for drama, ever

When we entered high school, we were still "the girls," constantly clumped together by our parents, boyfriends, teachers, and even our friends. As babies, my mom had bracelets made for us with our names to ensure we were easily differentiated. As pre-teens, it didn't matter, because we were considered a unit.

I wanted to look more like Traci. Even with all of us having dark hair (which we always kept the same length) and the same light eyes, I never thought we looked alike. There were only a couple of times when I would not know who was who. Once, I walked down the stairs toward a full-length mirror and thought I was looking at Michelle, but it was me!

With pictures especially, no one could determine who was who; even I couldn't. But as we got older, I felt we evolved. Traci was prettiest and the most exotic; she had an innate sex appeal. Men were always instantly attracted to her. She would always have the perfect make-up and dressed herself nicely. Michelle didn't care about any of that; we called her Urnavurna. She was granola and a bit of a hippie. Ultimately, she was more interested in art. I was athletic, and even though I was in great shape, I always had body image issues.

No one understood how we could fight one minute, and then the next minute love each other. It was always two against one. It was as though we had our own language. My stories were the beginning and the end. If anyone wanted to know the details in the middle, they'd ask Michelle.

People ask, "What's it like to be a triplet?"

I always answer, "I don't know what's it like to be an individual."

Find what makes you special and build on it

There became an interesting type of competition because we looked so much alike to others. I knew I had to figure out how to stand out somehow. I had to do things differently in order to survive. I couldn't stand one more person saying "the girls."

What's different about being a multiple birth person is that we share a lot, but have very different personalities. People didn't get that. It's like we were a freak show when the three of us were together. The stares were always an issue, people ogling us wherever we went. And we would each handle it differently.

And then there were the ridiculous questions . . .

Do you share a brain? When she's hurt, are you? Do you share the same dreams? When she's sick, do you get sick?

Can you tell each other apart? Can your mom tell you apart? Can your husbands and boyfriends tell you apart? If you don't like a guy, does he like the other sister?

It would make me laugh when someone would ask Michelle if we were triplets, which is already ridiculous, because we look identical. She would be completely deadpan and say, "No," then walk away, leaving the person perplexed. I'd smile from ear to ear.

I wanted to stand out so people would say, "She is Kym! She is not 'the girls.'" But through all things good and evil, I was glad I had people there for me.

My quest to be unique had always been a constant in my life, both as a businesswoman as well as an individual. Being a triplet encompassed friends, family, boyfriends, husbands, business; it was all mixed in to it.

I never had my own birthday. Whether my sisters were physically there or not, on my birthday it was never mine alone; I shared it with two other people. When we were together, sharing our birthday, it didn't feel like it was *my* day. But then, if my sisters weren't with me . . . there was a huge void.

Two

DECONSTRUCTED

For years it was a convenient cruise down the 101 freeway, thirteen miles between my dad and mom's houses. But after spending day outings in Malibu, George decided he really liked the area and that it would provide a better life for us, so he bought a place on Grasswood Street in Point Dume.

We didn't want to live in Malibu. We didn't want to leave our friends in Tarzana. But George sold the house in the valley, and we had no choice but to follow. It was the summer before starting junior high. The property had an old burned-out house with a stunning view. The plan was he would renovate the house and bring us over.

Unfortunately, the Point Dume house was nowhere near ready for us to move into by the time the Tarzana house closed escrow. Instead of moving into the new home we had been seduced into accepting, we had to move into a painfully small trailer in Paradise Cove, a sort of funky mobile home village along the coast. The seven of us squeezed into a two-room trailer for what seemed like an eternity. There were three pre-teen girls, one older and one younger brother, and our parents . . . with one bathroom. My deteriorating attitude had plummeted to the point where I hated everybody.

The instability that came with the false promise of our new home, only to have been let down and shorthanded, made me never want to promise anything unless I knew I could deliver. It was a silent pact for me from that time forward—I would absolutely deliver on my promises. That intent was a driving force in all my businesses. I was adamant, one might even say compulsive, that we deliver my clothing lines on schedule, or if I said something was going to be done, it got done.

I remember one of my first clothing businesses was called I Like This. I had gone to an open call for designers at the clothing store Contempo Casuals. Every Friday their buyers would check out new designers' samples and give you an order if they liked the clothes. I had gotten my designs in there.

The shipping company I was using got the delivery date wrong to ship the garments, and if a shipping company delivers even a day late, the store can cancel the order. My order was due the next day, so I was there all night to pack the boxes of clothes, put them in my truck, and the next morning I delivered them personally so they would get there on time.

Finally, the fateful day came when we could move into our Point Dume house. There was this beautiful stained glass on the front door, with a spiral staircase that went up to my parents' room, where the view was ridiculously expansive. You could see whales when they migrated, and the long kitchen looked out onto the yard, where George would plant his bonsai trees. But it was our room that took my breath away. It was as though magical angel dust was released when my mom and George opened our bedroom door, revealing our very own triplet oasis. For the first time in months I smiled. We all did. It had three cute, sectioned-off cubicles, each with a bed, a closet, and its own dresser, with a fun seating area. We were deliriously happy with it.

I had been battling with fitting in, never feeling pretty, and was having weight issues (even though I was incredibly fit), so finally having a place to call my own grounded me. It was a godsend.

It was a lesson for me that, just as I got to my wit's end—and feeling as though it was my darkest hour—waiting for that next moment could bring a much-needed respite. Getting my room was one example, but that was a recurring theme in my life.

We were enrolled in Malibu Park Junior High. Once we started attending, we began making friends. Malibu had such an eclectic group of kids growing up out there. The school register read like a page out of *People* magazine. We were really close with Chris Cortazzo, who would become one of the most well-known real estate agents in Malibu; we had sleepovers with Susan Traylor, who later became a great actress and producer; Amy Bosling (who later became Baer), the daughter of Tom Bosley (Mr. Cunningham from *Happy*

Hold on for that next moment of respite

Days) who would go on to be president of CBS Films, was always at our house; I would go over to Steve McQueen's when Ali McGraw was there, and when I dated Chad McQueen, their son, for a minute; Chris Penn (Sean Penn's brother) and Chad Lowe (Rob Lowe's brother) were always with us on the beach; Charlie Estevez (Martin Sheen's son) and my brother were best friends, and having moved to Grasswood, our backyard butted up to the Sheens' backyard, where Martin had built a baseball field for Charlie. I didn't play, but we whiled away the hours watching; Sharre Jacobi always threw great parties; Jennifer Grant, the daughter of Cary Grant and Dyan Cannon, would be around; and one of my best friends to this day, Holly Robinson Peete, sang in my brother's band. We would all hang out on the private beach, Little Dume, where you had to have a key to get in. We would stay there for hours. I was finally settling in and realizing it was a cool life in Malibu.

Even Rob Lowe commented about our Halloween escapades in those days in his book *Stories I Only Tell My Friends*, giving details of the burning tires that were thrown down the hills, and Martin Sheen, who had recently returned from making *Apocalypse Now*, coming out wearing commando fatigues with a baseball bat to get control of the craziness.

There was something so surreal about going to local parties and having celebrities like Michael Jackson, Barbra Streisand, Eddie Murphy, John Peters, and Larry Hagman partying among us in plain view.

As we got older, there needed to be self-regulating rules for us girls. We would monitor each other's time spent on the phone, in the bathroom, and always whose turn it was to clean up. I have always liked things in a very particular way, so being organized came easy, even necessary, to me, and was not a chore in my mind.

Whichever one of us met a new friend first got dibs on that person. We would get into fights when one of us would speak to a friend of another, saying, "What are you doing talking to them?! That's my friend!"

Although we had made a kind of pact in not sharing friends or boyfriends, we did share just about everything else. For years, George would take us skiing and the three of us would stand at the bottom of the chair lift. He would buy us one ticket, because we were identical and the ticket takers wouldn't notice as we took turns wearing Michelle's orange down jacket with a furry hood onto the lift. He saved a ton of money on lift tickets through the years.

While trying to generate more business, George, a personal injury attorney, got in trouble for ambulance chasing. It was becoming too common an occurrence by attorneys at the time and frowned upon, so the judge made him an example. Or at least that's the story I got at the time. I still don't know for sure.

For a moment he considered moving us to Costa Rica rather than going to jail. We almost went until our dad voiced his objection rather adamantly.

"Absolutely not! You are *not* taking my kids!"

In the end, we stayed put. For my dad, it was bad enough driving to Malibu; a plane flight to Costa Rica was out of the question.

George had to go to jail. It was a minimum-security prison, but it ignited his disregard for his own legal profession.

During his incarceration, my mom would drive us out to see him at the prison. We would walk through security, feeling the weight of his actions, sitting with him at a lunch table and feeling conspicuous amongst the other families, as mom gave him whatever present she had brought him that visit. He would work hard at making us feel comfortable, telling us stories and keeping it light. I was preoccupied with my surroundings and wondered what the other men had done wrong.

Three months later, George was released. Our bat mitzvah had to be rescheduled mid-preparation when he was locked up, so we were finally able to have our ceremony. And it was well worth waiting for; George invited the entire seventh grade class to attend. It was a raucous party with all our friends.

We three girls all climbed up to the Bimah together at Temple Judea in the Valley to finally read our part of the Torah. Each of us, standing nervous but proud, took a section to recite. After, the whole family and our many friends celebrated together there at the temple. We had lots of food, and everyone was dancing and singing. We girls were all in heaven, it was so much fun. And the cherry on the cake for us was that, the next day, we were taken to Hawaii on holiday.

There was also the bonus of no longer having to lie about George being away in jail as my friends asked about his whereabouts, which was a relief.

Independence

In high school, I was coming into my own fashion sense. The one thing I had to set me apart from my sisters was that I had my own sense of style.

With fashion, it's all about first impressions, so when you're out there wearing something interesting and fashion forward, it differentiates you within a crowd and sets you apart. It certainly did for me.

I could go to a vintage store and put a paisley with a plaid, wear the pieces together, and everyone would compliment me on my outfits. I constantly got fantastic responses, so I felt as if I was on to something. It challenged me to continually try new combinations to impress the other students. No matter what I wore, after I took it off and put it in the laundry hamper, Traci would retrieve each piece and wear the exact same outfit the next day. That was my first inkling that I had a talent. As it became more distinct, fashion became my solace. I had found something that separated me from not only my sisters, but everyone else as well.

When I couldn't find something I liked, I would buy something close and reconstruct it. Starting in junior high, my sisters and I would go to the old Vans store and I would take a pair of tennis shoes and dye them with tea bags, scribble on them, use RID dye, and try twisting the material to see how it would turn out. It fed me. Like so many other designers, I found my voice in fashion!

If someone copies you—feel flattered

We drove a beat-up yellow VW bug convertible with a stick shift twenty miles to get to Santa Monica High School. The three of us took turns driving, depending on who didn't do their homework the night before. And because of traffic, no matter what time we left, we always missed first period.

Winter was brutal. When it rained, we would have to drive a forty-eight-mile circuitous route to get to school. We'd all cry to our mom, "Seriously? Can't we just miss today?!" She would hand us our bag lunches as an answer.

I had started playing volleyball in junior high and had gotten really good, so in high school I joined the Varsity team. Although I didn't take the offer to have a volleyball scholarship in college, I was thankful for the competitive training the sport gave me.

Through volleyball I learned how to work as part of a team, but also to push myself to be the best individually; a healthy sense of competition; have confidence in winning; and how to lose gracefully and get over the loss. I had no idea how poignant those lessons would be for me, especially in business, in the years to come.

Team sports help create business leaders

Traci was the smarter one in school. One time we switched classes; she went into math class for me so she could take my math test because I wasn't prepared for it. The next day, the teacher called me up to her desk, holding the test with a red "100" circled. Pointedly, she gazed at me from under her rimmed glasses and said, "Really, Kym?"

The question hung heavy in the air. After a moment of crushing inference that I had lied, I came clean. "It was Traci!"

She cocked her head. "Yes, it was." Somewhat amused, she let me retake the test.

Traci was dating guys already out of high school. Michelle did, too, but she was Urnavurna, so didn't have the same sexual magnetism. I was the one more my age. Playing volleyball all the time, so much that I never had time for a best friend. I was so into sports, and then I started going out with a high school football player.

There was a constant stream of parties in the colony and in Serra Retreat. My parents traveled quite often, and they would leave my mom's mom to watch us. We would stay downstairs with Charlie and Sharre for hours, just hanging out before going out to one party or another.

Throughout high school, we sisters were a force to be reckoned with wherever we went. We were built-in best friends.

"You're friends with the triplets?" I would hear kids coo in an impressed, hushed tone as we walked through the hallways. It was unusual to see a triplet, and I understood that, but after a while it created a distrust in why someone was a friend. It put up a guardedness that only grew more significant through the years.

Acting Years

We had gone on the occasional acting audition from a young age. From the time George saw us as children, we were groomed for performing as "the triplets," whether in film or on TV. He felt there was an opportunity for us, whether we wanted it or not.

George had always wanted to be our manager of sorts, wanting to oversee our acting career. He loved us, very much, but it became an opportunity for him.

In high school we started doing a lot of commercials and then got involved in TV shows and movies: *Star Trek*, *Dream On*, *Big Business*, and a pilot with Charlie Sheen. By then, my aversion to auditions was seriously mounting. I never liked being stared at, and unfortunately for me, that was part of the mandate of that career choice. We worked on a *Charles in Charge* episode in our early twenties. I didn't want to do it, so Traci played not only her part, but mine as well.

Traci wanted to be an actress, so we all acquiesced and accompanied her to the auditions and jobs. But it was the worst thing for me. I was too impatient to sit around and wait for the casting directors to let us into a room for the producers and director to stare at us, telling me what I could and could not do. Then comment with the obvious, "You're too ethnic." Hello, Jews from Malibu! There was always something they would have an issue with: not thin enough, pretty enough, outgoing enough, etc. It all made me want to tell them, "Fuck you."

The worst was that we had to dress alike. I hated that. We would drive to auditions in the convertible, dressed in our identical outfits, and people would almost get in car accidents, craning their heads to catch a glimpse. I had my own style, so to have to regress back into looking the same disgusted me.

Most of the time we would fight all the way there, then audition and be *on*. After our audition, we would walk out smiling and laughing, then the moment we were back in the car we would pick up the fight where we had left off. It got to be comical.

When we did get booked, I felt it important to do a good job. I wanted to further Traci's dream. But I wasn't in control of my own destiny, and that was hard for me.

We would find ourselves on casting calls that would turn into a casting couch situation. The casting director would just about drool, "How about a ménage a quatre?"

You could see it on his face, the excitement at the idea of having the three of us in some compromising position. At that point, I was very "enthusiastic" about using my voice. Shockingly, we didn't get any of those jobs.

When we were on *Charles in Charge*, they wanted the three of us to come in for a callback wearing booty shorts. The problem was the wardrobe didn't call for booty shorts. We didn't feel comfortable, and if the part didn't call for it, why do it? We were already in competition in subtle ways amongst the three of us.

We went home and decided as a threesome not to do that. When we came back, we were wearing something else. The producers were not happy.

When they wanted me to do a kissing part with the lead actor Scott Biao, I had Traci do it instead. And why not? She wanted to be the actress, not me!

As triplets, our whole lives have been about our being on display, feeding people's curiosity. The idea of adding a gratuitous reason to be gawked at was my nightmare.

To this day, there is an ambivalence that runs through my life regarding the three of us. If there are professional photographers snapping pictures of just me, it doesn't make me comfortable. However, if the three of us are together as the subject, I feel safe, so it doesn't bother me. But then, I don't enjoy being clumped together, either. It's a constant inner dialogue that happens with me when it comes to the three of us.

Although I knew acting was not for me, I did know I was going to be something big. I could feel that I had a whole lot of energy, and I knew I was an out of the box thinker. Even at that point it was quite obvious I didn't like to conform. I was still young, so wasn't sure how to utilize my energy best, but I knew fashion was calling to me.

We were in our teens when George started *Faces International*. Our mom was still a stay-at-home mom, watching helplessly as George became more engrossed in the entertainment industry. As the business grew, so, too, did George's narcissism. Soon, his offhanded comments became more caustic. He was no longer the dad that I loved and needed so badly, the gentle man who asked us if he could enter into our lives to be with our mom.

So, when George remarked in passing, "Wives are like whores if they don't work," I took it to heart.

That was a huge statement to say about your wife, a woman, and my mother. It rattled every atom in my body. I was clear: *That is not going to be me. I never want to be dependent on a man.* There are pivotal moments in childhood, and that was a big one for me.

Faces International was a magazine distributed internationally to agents, managers, and production companies as a vehicle for actors to get their faces seen in the entertainment industry. It became instantly popular, plunking him right into the center of the entertainment industry.

George was married to my mom for twenty-three years, and then he, like my father, had an affair and left. It was a betrayal down to my core, because in each case the men didn't just leave her, they left us.

When all you know of men is that they will leave their wives for other women, it becomes molecular. I didn't ever want to put myself in a position to be hurt like that.

Because of my tumultuous upbringing, I wanted to be completely self-sufficient. I never wanted a man to tell me what I could and could not spend my money on, and more significantly, no man would ever get close enough to break my heart.

Three

OVERSTOCKED

I met Mark Burnett, the creator of the later renowned television empires *Survivor*, *The Voice*, *Shark Tank*, etc., when I was a hostess at a local restaurant called Alice's in Malibu. He would come in frequently with a bunch of guys; I was taken by his British accent and style right away. He was new to Los Angeles, having moved from east London, where he was raised. I thought he was gorgeous. He had joined the British Army and became a Section Commander in the Parachute Regiment. Although it had been a couple of years since he had been in the military, his body was incredibly fit. He also had a sense of wonder and excitement to him.

Mark was game for anything; at the time I met him he was working as a nanny. We started dating and I was enamored with him, but I think he was even more enamored with me. I was a girl from California, from Malibu even, who had style and mingled with the rich and famous.

The twenty-seven miles of Malibu has always been considered the land of celebrities. He was now a part of that echelon of people. His eyes were opened wide with the possibilities.

I had graduated high school and desperately wanted to be in the garment business. My sisters and I were finally starting to become autonomous. Traci had gone on to work as a hairstylist and create a makeup company. Michelle was taking massage therapy classes and later became an acupuncturist.

Mark and I rented a loft in Santa Monica on 4th Street and Raymond Avenue. We would have what we called Sunday Funday, going down to Venice Beach. Back then it was a long strip of boardwalk along the sea with roller skaters galore and hippies selling crystals and incense.

I had an idea that I would like to sell T-shirts on the boardwalk. Clothes weren't being sold yet, so I thought I would find out who the landowner was, call him, and ask if I could rent some space.

Clothing designers sell their overages and damages, which are just slightly imperfect clothes. My idea was to buy damaged T-shirts and garment dye them my own colors and then sew material shapes on them to cover any holes.

I asked George and Mom if I could borrow three hundred dollars and promised to pay them back. No doubt they assumed that day would be in the very distant future, if ever.

I went downtown to the mart where the showrooms were, having never been downtown before and certainly never alone. Up until that time, I rarely went anywhere by myself.

Terrified, I started knocking on doors. But, before they could shut the door on me, I would manage to blurt out, "Hi! Can I buy your overages or irregulars?!"

Some people were nice, some shut the door on me, some were snobby, and some were downright mean. Back then people didn't even think to sell overages and damages, so they didn't understand my idea. Initially it was frowned upon, as their thinking was, if they're selling to Neiman's and Saks, they didn't want the T-shirt found on the boardwalk for half the price. But it didn't deter me; there was a thrill to the chase.

When I finally got someone to say "Yes" to me, I was totally intimidated by the next step, which was to rummage through their warehouse to find the T-shirts I deemed quality enough to buy. As nervous as I was, my pride kept pushing me forward. I believed in my idea.

I remember calling Mark from a payphone, saying, "I'm across the street from a dye house. I'm going to dye a bunch of T-shirts."

He told me I was wasting my money. But I had a hunch. The T-shirts that had holes or tears, I would use a crisscross or bar tack stitching, or cut out stars, squares, and hearts from interesting fabrics to sew patches over the holes.

Mark was not the only one who said I shouldn't sell the T-shirts—everyone thought it was a waste of my time, which just made me that much more driven. I love a challenge.

I bought the damaged T-shirts for five dollars each, put up some racks and umbrellas on the Venice boardwalk, and sold the repurposed T-shirts for twenty to thirty dollars each. By my first weekend I'd sold everything. To my stepdad's surprise, I paid the three-hundred-dollar loan back the very next week.

Find strength in believing

To the Next Level

Michelle started working for me, and then Mark realized the success I was having and the money making possibilities, and came on board to sell. He, Michelle, and I would hawk the T-shirts in this little six-by-nothing space on the boardwalk. It would be packed the whole day, and by nightfall we would have nothing left. We were exhausted but enthralled by the experience. Each morning I would go downtown again with the profits we made to buy more T-shirts.

Within the year I doubled my space in Venice, opened a place in Northridge, and one at Cal State LA. I went to each of the colleges and said, "If you let me sell in the quad at the college, I'll give you a percentage and pay you rent." They had me sign an insurance waiver, and I was off and running.

I started doing private clothing parties. In addition, every other Friday at the California Mart downtown, they would have shoe sales in the basement and we would sell there. Poor Michelle would spend all the money she made every day buying clothes from all the other vendors. I have a shoe crush, so I definitely spent some money on shoes.

I eventually added a place in Long Beach and the Rodium Swap Meet in Torrance, as well as the Rose Bowl. For the Rose Bowl I would have to leave by 4:00 a.m. to be set up by 6:00, along with all the other vendors. All my spaces were selling like crazy.

As exhilarating as it was, it was a lot of labor! You had to set up at the location, lug in the clothes, set up the umbrellas, and organize the rack to display the T-shirts, which took an hour. At the end of the day, you had to repack the car, drive home, and unpack the car, easily another hour. You're building a store everywhere you go. My turnkey store was everywhere I went. A few times a week I had to schlep downtown from Santa Monica to get more T-shirts and organize the dying houses. And at the end of the day, after everything else, I had to do my accounting.

As we ramped up, I had to find new manufacturers to buy T-shirts from, because I had sold all the overages from the other relationships I had made.

My future husband, Jeff Lubell, was twenty-nine at the time and married to Mindy. We all knew each other peripherally from other friends. Mindy had a twin sister, go figure, whose husband had a clothing company called Us Boys. I asked him if I could buy his damages. As it turned out, he had thousands, and I would buy them all on a regular basis.

By the end of each weekend, I couldn't wait for everybody to get together to count out all the money we made. I had six places running and was making fifty thousand dollars cash a month at nineteen years old. Some days I didn't want to do it. I had a drawer full of cash, I was kind of bummed that I couldn't just go lay on a beach somewhere. But I would once again pack up and head out. I was unstoppable, and the icing on the cake was that Mark, whom I had been living with all along, now wanted to marry me!

Before the wedding, we went to England for a month. It was completely liberating for me to have Mark's undivided attention away from my sisters and other family members.

Oftentimes, when my sisters and I are together, it detracts from everything else. So, when not with them, Mark had to talk to me, be with me. Mark always wanted to talk about business with my stepdad, too, so this gave him fewer distractions, with me reaping the benefits.

He took me to Dagenham, the East End of London where he's from, and showed me around the rest of the city. I was charmed by the place, and it was so romantic. He took me to hear the underground music, see the fashion, revel in the art. It all made me bubble with creativity. After having absorbed the history, architecture, and style of Britain, I was inspired and couldn't wait to get home and design. But first, I was to get married. In order to do that, Mark and I had to take a six-week course through the temple. The lessons intrigued Mark, and I believe became handy later in his life when he produced the mini-series *The Bible*.

In the late eighties, on August fourteenth, with an ocean view and gorgeous weather, we said our vows in my mom and George's Point Dume home.

I had asked my stepdad to walk me down the aisle. I could forgive his disrespectful comments over the years in that joyous moment. He had always been the man I would refer to as a father. My biological dad was furious.

"How can you do that, Kym? That's embarrassing to me."

But at that point I wasn't there to take care of his feelings; he had never taken care of mine.

The difference between Brits and Americans was immediately visible. At our ceremony, hats were worn by every woman on the groom's side, whereas on the bride's side, not a one. A lot of his family had flown out for the event, and we had a hell of a party. It was a stunning day.

Mark had invited Jeff Lubell to the wedding, so he was there as a guest.

Even though Mark and I were having such a special day, I had an inkling, even at that time, that I wished it was Jeff who was meeting me at that altar. It was just a twinge of a feeling, and I knew it was wrong, so I immediately pushed the thought away. It was Mark and I taking the plunge, and that was what I focused on.

Growing up, I had shared everything with my sisters—our eye color, hair, birthdays—now I finally had something of my own. That was what I found in Mark.

My family paid for Mark and I to have an extravagant honeymoon. We took a car and went all over Europe. We started in Paris, then drove to the south of France and all the way back around again. It was such a romantic trip. A girl from Malibu and boy from the East End were staying in lavish castles, Hotel Maurice in Paris, and one of the most beautiful hotels on the beach overlooking the yachts in Cannes. In seeing the places through Mark's cockney, sarcastic, and witty perspective, it made for an amazing adventure. We left Europe with a deep appreciation for each other. Unbeknownst to me, I had become pregnant during that trip.

After we got back, I was feeling frustrated. Even though I was doing well financially, I wanted to do more than to sell T-shirts on the boardwalk and at swap meets. I get bored easily, so I'm always trying new things. I was jonesing for some new challenges.

I went to Santa Monica College and enrolled in business courses. I had been offered a volleyball scholarship when I graduated high school, but I just didn't see myself going to

San Luis Obispo. I wanted to further my design career in Los Angeles.

Creatives, build up your business acumen

I ensconced myself in fashion and school. At the time, I knew that the creative side of my brain was fertile. So, instead of focusing solely on design classes, I took some business classes to harness that side of my brain. I knew that being creative without having business acumen to back it up wouldn't get me far in the industry, and I had big aspirations.

A $400,000 Building

Our building on 4th Street and Raymond Avenue came up for sale, and I bought it for four hundred thousand dollars. A few weeks later I had the opportunity to sell it back to the guy who sold it to me. He was sorry he'd gotten rid of it and thought he had made a mistake. I sold it back to him at the new market value of seventy thousand more, which he gladly paid.

It triggered the idea of my selling real estate, so I started studying for my real estate license. We took the profit from the building sale and Mark and I promptly bought a house in Malibu.

When Mark came home one night, I flung open the door and blurted out, "I'm pregnant!" We were both really excited about having a baby.

Although our relationship didn't have that deep, passionate, soulful connection, we worked well together and had a mutual respect and love that felt like enough.

When I had a miscarriage at eleven weeks, we both kept moving forward with our lives together, but there was a sad elephant in the room.

When I did get my real estate license, my stepdad said to me, “You’re twenty years old, who’s going to buy a five-million-dollar house from you?”

That could be true, but if I listened to that, I wouldn’t have stayed true to my convictions, and my instincts had been steering me in the right direction. After getting my license, I realized quickly that as much as I loved real estate, I didn’t love being a realtor.

Mark and I started working for my stepdad at *Faces International*. I was working in the LA office in sales. Mark became vice president. Why he would become vice president, I don’t know. Because I brought him into the mix? Because he was a man? Because he knew secrets about my stepdad? Probably all of the above.

Stay true to your convictions

Mark began traveling around for the company and started having an affair with Dianne Valentine, who would later become his wife.

Mark didn’t think I looked at the credit card and hotel bills. I let them accumulate for a few months, and since he was vice president of the company, I could easily find out that the transaction amount wasn’t from the hotel he was supposed to be in.

Another time, he was supposed to be with his best friend Steven in the UK, who remained great friends with Mark. He was the best man at our wedding. When I would call to speak with Mark, it occurred to me that Steven was acting quite odd, and then when he would try to get ahold of Mark, he couldn't find him either. I think Mark wanted to be caught.

If you have a feeling about something, do your research. The truth always prevails.

After having accumulated information about the affair, I brought it to Mark's attention. He couldn't say "No." If he did, I would point to my evidence. "Oh really? Here is this, here is that, here is this." Then Mark said the words that would shake my world.

"Your dad knew."

They had secrets on each other, because George was also having affairs that my mom was unaware of.

That was the next level of pain.

I learned what betrayal looked like. I was George's favorite. I emulated and respected him. That was the beginning of the end of my relationship with my stepdad. It was also the end for Mark and me.

Mark made his entrée into producing television. He had a lot of tenacity. I always saw that in him. He wanted to be better, not just the boy from Dagenham. He saw an idea with an eco-challenge and made it into an empire. He was a smart and shrewd businessman who stayed true to his convictions.

I went on to create clothing companies. We split the proceeds of the sale on the house in Malibu and went our separate ways.

We were young, so as painful as it was in that moment, we have stayed friends to this day. Two of our kids were born on the same day at the same time, at the same hospital in Santa Monica. We didn't know the other was there. Those boys are now friends.

Four

GOODS AND DAMAGES

I first met Jeff Lubell when I was fifteen. He was ten years older and married. Although I thought he was kind of cute, I saw him simply as one of the beach bums.

It wasn't until I was selling the T-shirts that he really came into my life. I had just started up my first clothing company, Kymberly Suits You. As I mentioned, at the time, I was married to Mark and buying the T-shirts from Jeff's wife's sister and her husband.

After Mark and I split, Jeff and I ran into each other at a party George threw for *Faces International.* His events were always epic, and this was no different. There were five hundred actors, writers, producers, agents—anyone and everyone in entertainment was in attendance. I had a physical reaction when I saw Jeff. It was like love at first sight; it was completely visceral. His being at the party was so out of context I couldn't help but ask, "What are you doing here?"

It turned out that a mutual friend in entertainment had invited him. He looked at me differently because I was no longer the fifteen-year-old at the beach he'd met those many years ago, and now, I was no longer Mark's wife. However, he was still Mindy's husband . . . barely.

We fell deeply in love. It was a heavy-duty, real love that was blossoming during the downslide of his marriage, which was mutually headed for divorce. I felt badly about our having a relationship, but we were like a drug for each other. Jeff was selling fabrics and was still living with Mindy, which suited me fine, as I could keep him at arm's length. He would come to see me at my apartment in Westwood, which I shared with Traci. She was disgusted by the situation, but he and I were in love. He would send me flowers and buy me presents—he loved to shop for me.

It was not lost on me that no matter how I looked at it, I was entering into a relationship with a married man. It was a reckless act I had seen tear people and families apart. As much as I was scintillated by our being together, I could not push that aside.

A year after we started seeing each other, I moved alone to a small studio in a modern building on Swall Avenue in Beverly Hills. A couple of months after, Jeff showed up saying, "I did it. I left my wife."

To say I was somewhat anxious about those words is an understatement. I was twenty-three and had gotten out of my own marriage only a year before. I had even thought our relationship was so intoxicating and intense that once he left Mindy, it might just sizzle out. But there he was on my doorstep, and we just fit together. Mindy got remarried a couple of years after they'd divorced, which assuaged my guilt about her wellbeing. By then I was free to really absorb fully that this man was my soulmate, and we were meant to be together, and it was much more than just a fling.

Initially, I didn't want to get married again. I would have been fine just living together forever in a committed relationship. I had seen marriages that meant nothing, so for me, the commitment meant more than the piece of paper.

Jeff was selling fabric and I was still at *Faces International*, so we lived simply in our little studio apartment. We had no money, nothing to speak of really, but we were so happy together.

I didn't smoke pot, but Jeff loved it. I was in such a state of bliss that it never bothered me; it was just who he was. He was never a big drinker, so pot seemed nebulous in our relationship. Jeff was hard of hearing and didn't like to use a hearing aid, so I'm sure the neighbors thought I screamed at him a lot. I got used to speaking loudly—he didn't like people to know he couldn't hear.

When I got pregnant, Jeff reintroduced the conversation about marriage, "Kym, we will be together forever. I want you to marry me and take my name."

By then I was less defensive about it and truly believed we would live our lives out together. So we had an intimate ceremony with the family and a rabbi in Beverly Hills on Robertson. After, we all had pizza together. I wore a flowery frock because I had just started showing, so the virginal white was out.

We flew out to Hawaii for our honeymoon and stayed at the Grand Wailea in Hawaii with another couple, Arlene and Gary Treisman, who were also pregnant at the same time. Gary, as it turns out, would later play a pivotal role in getting True Religion to go public.

My first child, Jake, was born on March 16, 1993. He was wide-eyed and gorgeous and the love of my life. I loved being a mother. And Jeff was completely devoted to him.

I stopped working at *Faces International* to start my own clothing company called Get Into Trouble. Jeff's mom came to work for me, and we would answer the phone, "Get into trouble!" giving people a laugh. It was my first taste of running a business while being a mother. I was feeling good about being able to keep everything afloat, and the business was gaining traction.

We moved to a charming house on Butterfield Road in Rancho Park. I was busy with the baby and running the company. But not too busy to get pregnant again.

Ryan was a wonderfully happy accident. Born April 24, 1994, he was in and out of the hospital a lot with ear infections, and finally we had to take his adenoids out. All the while I was battling with postpartum depression and getting no real support for it, either from doctors or from Jeff. I was too busy with life and trying to press on and remain stoic and handle it all.

I was going to each doctor's appointment by myself, fearful for my child and upset at seeing him in pain. It was a daily debate whether to continue getting my clothing line out there or close it down to take care of the kids. Meanwhile, Jeff was at work and not involved in the day to day of the household.

It was helpful that I could bring the babies with me to the office. But it was hard to focus, even with Jeff's mom there, or a babysitter, whom I would bring in if I needed to take a meeting. I finally decided it was time to get a nanny a couple of days a week, and often I would bring everything home and work from there. It's amazing what a woman can accomplish with two babies.

Decisions, Decisions, Decisions

I was a new mother and very ambitious, and I believed wholeheartedly that I could do it all. So I tried to maintain everything and push forward on projects as I had done before having the kids. I am ultra-organized and efficient, so it worked for me to keep all the plates in the air. But when there was a kink in the plan, it played havoc on the day. And with Ryan's health, every day was touch and go. I felt pressure from all quadrants of my life; I knew it landed on me to make something happen. I couldn't find an answer for why Ryan had so many issues, so I had to go to different doctors. My overwhelming concern was making me lose sleep. Finally, I went to a homeopathic doctor, and on his recommendation, changed Ryan's whole diet.

But I was trying to juggle too much. There came a day when I finally hit a wall. I made the decision to close down the company so I could be with the boys and be a mom full time. They were my priority over any company, and I just found it was too much to do on my own. I needed a break and wanted to be with the boys. It is a decision I am glad I made, because it gave me the opportunity to find alternatives for Ryan, which were effective. It was a good decision.

I had two kids under thirteen months old. It was the most ecstatic, and the most exhausting, time of my life. Both Jeff and I were madly in love with them. Through all our drama, that was always the case.

During my closing down the company, Jeff wasn't very helpful. Maybe he was disappointed I wouldn't be bringing in money, or perhaps he thought I was making a bad decision to give up the company, but given the opportunity, I would do the same thing over again.

You find the fundamental differences in the man you marry when you have kids and you are fucking ass tired and need more help than you have. Those differences become even more glaring when you don't have money and you're struggling to make ends meet.

Jeff and I were both full tilt on all levels, which is a comfortable state for me to live in, as I generally work in warp speed. Jeff would always say, "Kym is a tornado; you either jump inside or she'll spit you out."

I don't have a lot of patience; if you can't follow my speed then I'm on to the next person, place, or thing.

With manufacturers, if I had to wait for them to give me an answer, I was done and moved on. There was always another solution. Good, bad, or indifferent, I work at a high speed. It's not an impulse; it is just my natural speed in life. As it happens, I don't go in the slow lane on the freeway either; I always go in the fast lane. I consider it proactive.

Jeff thought having kids helped make things better. I didn't necessarily disagree with that; I knew it could make it worse. But we shared in a desire to have another baby. We discussed it and said, "Yeah, let's do it!"

We were in a good place in our marriage, and there was no way I was going to be without that man. So we started working on getting me pregnant.

We had our third, Dylan. He was born April 26, 1997. It was again another love affair. I grew a new heart with each of my kids. There is a love I will always have for Jeff for giving me my children.

Now having a family, we thought we should get a bigger space. This time we found a house centrally located in Manhattan Beach.

I had my mojo back and was getting antsy for another company. Six months later, I started Bella Dahl. I took thirteen pairs of old Levi's and added cut-up kimonos on the bottom. It became a phenomenon.

Bella Dahl

Bella Dahl was a hit. It was fast and furious. Jake and Ryan were three and four at the time and in a fun little Jewish daycare. I had Dylan with me as I ran around buying canton fabric in Little India and dropping things off at manufacturers downtown and Fred Segal, a unique trendsetting store that houses individually, designer-owned boutiques inside. Dylan and I were thick as thieves. He was like Velcro. I took him everywhere with me. I would go downtown and research vintage jeans and explain to the manufacturers how I wanted the kimonos sewn on while he would rummage through the fabrics.

Before I left Rancho Park, I had hired a nanny, Lupe, who stayed with me for eleven years. She was my everything. The one solid person I could depend on in every situation.

When she started, I didn't speak a word of Spanish, and she didn't know any English. I started using Spanish phrase books so we could communicate. Hand signals would only go so far. With every year that passed, I became more fluent and, in time, I would only speak to her in Spanish. She had been my Spanish teacher. And, also, my trusted employee/sister to whom I could always turn for support. She and I are still very close.

Jeff saw Bella Dahl's potential and wanted to grow the business, so he brought in a finance company to fund the expansion. We had made a couple of million and now I needed money to grow, but the guys that he brought in basically stole the company from me. They stopped paying, and in doing so, leveraged the company from under me. It was a dire situation that had me in court for a year. I had worked hard on Bella Dahl, there had been a lot of sweat equity put into it, so to have it taken away was heartbreaking. And worse yet, it created in me a resentment toward Jeff.

After the loss of Bella Dahl, Jeff and I called Paul Guez, a major financier for jean companies. We told him about the Bella Dahl situation, though most in the industry were already aware of our story. He invited us to come under his umbrella. We called Paul on a Friday and we went to work on the Monday. I wanted to get past what had happened with Bella Dahl. We created Hippie Jeans for Paul.

I was the designer and Jeff would source the fabric for the prototypes.

Levi's became interested in my designing for them. I met with them up in San Francisco three or four times. It was tempting, as I have such respect for the brand, but they were not the right fit for me.

Their decision-making process was slow and ponderous, which worked for them, but I don't have that kind of constitution. It also meant I would have had to uproot my family and move up north. I ultimately walked away from that opportunity.

We booked three million dollars in sales for Paul, but because he had enough designs and samples from us, he didn't want to pay us any longer. Even though he continued selling the brand, we weren't getting money from him, so I had no choice but to go design for Rampage and Laundry by Shelli Segal.

Life's too short to take a job not right for you

The Birth of True Religion

We lived in a half-million-dollar house in Manhattan Beach with a hefty mortgage, leased two cars, had three kids (two of whom were in an expensive preschool), and a full-time housekeeper. In losing Hippie, maintaining our lifestyle, and now putting money into our newest venture, a jeans company we wanted to start up called True Religion, we were seriously losing grip on our finances. Jeff and I wanted to do our own thing. It made sense for us to utilize both our skills to create something together. It was a world that we both knew well. We wanted this incarnation of a company to be the right clothes, at the right time, with the right people.

But first, I needed to get our house in order. I was so intent on getting back on financial track that on top of working for Rampage and Shelli Segal, I took up doing weekend clothing parties. They were fun. We would call all our friends, invite everyone we knew, make cards and put them in mailboxes, invite the mothers of the kids' preschool to a great party, where I was selling clothes. It was reminiscent of what I had done in the Venice days.

Once we had a little nest egg again, Jeff thought, "My wife is working, we have a little saved and a house." He decided to take a sabbatical for three months from doing anything to do with clothing. He spent time with the kids, but felt he needed a rest, so he went back to his beach days and hung out on the beach. We had Lupe, so there was someone to watch the kids, so he had carte blanche to do nothing.

We seemed to be okay. But before we knew it, the bills started piling up, mortgages weren't getting paid, and we needed to start putting more serious money toward True Religion. We had found a warehouse in El Segundo and wanted to start hiring employees.

I was working so much, and being a mom in my off hours, that I had entrusted Jeff with the finances. I wasn't paying attention as our financial situation was becoming dire.

Soon our savings was gone. We had put everything we had into the company. We needed to pay salaries and the El Segundo warehouse rent, and suddenly we were mortgaged to the hilt, maxed out on our credit cards, and had to take a second mortgage on the house. But Jeff and I were committed to working together, forging ahead, and making True Religion work.

Five

PRODUCTIVE BY DESIGN

As impressive as True Religion had become by 2005, it certainly did not start out that way. In fact, when True Religion was first started, it was *extraordinarily* difficult to get traction. The years leading up to that thrilling summer of success were fraught with frustration and disappointments. It was a real rags to riches story.

I was still working at Rampage and Laundry during the day to support the family when we launched the company in 2002. I had to be downtown at nine o'clock to start my day at Rampage's offices. I'd finish around four and drive to City of Commerce to start designing Laundry for Shelli Segal through the night. That lasted a good four months until I left Shelli Segal; Paula Schneider was the president of Laundry and believed in my vision of doing something on my own. But I continued working for Rampage while we ramped up True Religion in earnest.

Thankfully, I have two sisters who look just like me (smile), Jeff, my mom, and Lupe, to help care for the kids.

But I had to take care of the family financially. I had no choice. I slotted in meetings to deal with the reps about the line during the week and would take time off to fly out to New York to go to the big apparel shows.

I was vice president of True Religion and creative director of Women's as well as being in charge of opening retail stores. It was a strategic move to make Jeff the president and CEO of our start-up, as he could be contacted at any time, whereas I could not while working at the other companies. He was also freer to get to El Segundo on a moment's notice, where I was trying to maintain my focus with the other designers on their lines and not let my frazzled existence interfere with my jobs.

It was so all-encompassing that I was more than willing to have Jeff take control when I wasn't there. I trusted him with my life. There was nothing I wouldn't do for him. And even though we were both so ensconced in trying to make the company work, we somehow were thriving on the excitement of what this company had the potential to be.

We brought on Charles Lesser, who I wasn't sure would be a good CFO for the company, but Jeff advocated for Charles and felt he had good insight. Charles had been the CFO of Weider Sporting Goods and increased their profit, so Jeff felt confident he could be helpful with True Religion. I did think he probably knew finances, but I also wasn't blind; this guy was no friend of mine. I acquiesced to keep Jeff happy.

We also brought on a tried and true production manager, Gonzalo, whom I did believe would be a friend to me and would work for the good of the company, and not just Jeff.

It was a whirlwind of a day, every day, at our house. There was momentum, but things were not happening fast enough. We needed to find investors and make a splash. Time was running out.

Buying expensive denim, payroll, and now needing to pay for five thousand garments to be sewn—it was too much, and we were wildly in debt to the tune of two hundred fifty thousand dollars. We couldn't afford our mortgage payments anymore, so we had to let the house go. Soon after that, we sold the car.

In the beginning, there were quite a few people who dropped the ball, almost sabotaging the company. It seemed so political. And unfortunately, our initial sales reps, whom I loved, didn't understand denim and how to sell it. I was at all the trade shows, having to sell with them, explaining to the buyers what it was that was so special about our brand. It was daunting to have it hang on my shoulders.

The words of my dad resounded in my head, from when he and my stepmom had sat Mark Burnett and I down before we got married.

"Neither one of you are going to make as much money as we make, because neither of you have a really solid career. You need to figure out a back-up plan," he said.

They didn't say it to be hurtful; it was more the talk of concerned parents. My dad was an attorney and my stepmom a nurse practitioner; their lives were traditional. At that moment, in retrospect, I wondered if they had given that speech to the wrong guy. Perhaps it should have been Jeff they sat down with, offering those words of advice on having a Plan B.

We ended up borrowing money from my mom and landing our posse in a hotel in Hermosa Beach, where we stayed until we could organize a rental. I wasn't sleeping and was so down and out and so depressed, that everything I did felt like it was weighted and exhausting in every area of life. The worst part was I had no energy for the kids, which made my guilt unbearable. Working those long hours on all fronts left me exhausted, and as happy as I was to see my three boys, the energy I had for them was very little at the time.

We had hit rock bottom. But even in that lowest moment, we still had this uncanny need to hold true to our conviction to continue with True Religion. We believed so wholeheartedly in our new brand and had come too far to turn back—not that we had anything to turn back to at that point. There was no Plan B for us. The only thing we could do was keep forging ahead.

What I did have this time around was a stronger knowledge of how to make sure we didn't lose control of the company. This time, having gone through lawsuits, mergers, buyouts, and the like, I was better versed in how the financing structures should be set up to maintain control of the shares. I was not going to let anyone take our company again.

We had opened our warehouse in El Segundo and were manufacturing in Gardena with Jeff Rudus, who later became owner of J Brand. Then we found Jana, a well-known sales agent. She knew the denim business, had an incredible aesthetic, and was unstoppable when it came to selling a line. In one sweep, we found another manufacturer downtown and begged Jana to be our rep. That was the trifecta. We were finally off and running—well, walking at least.

It was 2003, we had made five thousand jeans, and to pay for it, we maxed out one of our last credit cards that still had some credit available. The idea was to start with a men's jean and follow it soon after with a woman's. I had always thought women would want to wear a boyfriend pant, and I was right. Ultimately, they most certainly did.

The Jew Bu

From day one, I was of the mindset that we should keep everything in Los Angeles. All my previous companies were manufactured in Los Angeles, and I felt strongly True Religion should be, too. The issue with that was it made the jeans more expensive to manufacture. I knew it would be more of a struggle with labor at minimum wage rather than going overseas, but that seemed well worth it, and the pants were beautifully put together. The details of our pants were so specific that it was a lot easier when we could watch what was happening day by day.

When you manufacture in the same city you live in, it is right in front of you; you can see it. Generally, if it were being made in India or China, by the time it came back it could be all wrong and we would be back to the drawing board.

If something is wrong and the manufacturer is where you live, you can fix it in a day or a couple days, not another month out. You get to watch it all come together, and at the same time feel good that you are having an active impact in keeping your local economy afloat.

Everything that we wanted to do in the beginning, at every turn, everybody said no. Everybody. They said the pockets were too big, they didn't understand the choice of the twisted seam, and they didn't like the big stitches. Nor did they understand why the price had to be so expensive at over two hundred fifty dollars a pair, and the label was a debate to be had in every conversation.

Anytime you put a religious symbol up on a label, it is up for a debate.

The Buddha is a big symbol. Japan didn't want us to put it on the label, and Neiman Marcus didn't like it, but the label had meaning to us.

The logo came very organically, and we really felt strongly that it fit our vision. I called myself a Jew Bu because I was into eastern medicine. Jeff had always loved acoustic guitars. When we were thinking about the label, we thought how cool it would be to have a Buddha playing a guitar and seat numbers giving a concert stadium feel, something relatable throughout the world. We were not willing to budge on the look.

There was so much more to this jean as a whole: There are specialized seams, contour waistbands, and stitching that is expensive. It adds up. It wasn't being done thoughtlessly—everything I put on the jean was intentional. The stitching was expensive so that it would last through a kazillion washes. And then there was the denim that was chosen;

it was an expensive denim. But it was important to me. It was important for that jean. Ironically, it was the cost of the jean that created the buzz.

No one had ever seen such an expensive jean before, and there was the idea that if you could afford such an expensive pair of jeans, it meant something about who you were and what you were worth. Anyone who saw True Religion jeans on someone knew how much they cost, and it made a statement.

I believe with everything I do or have, that I get what I pay for. I wanted to be the Levi of our time. Levi jeans were known for quality, but our brand was also cool. It would be a product that would last years and only get better with time.

True Religion was going to be the better choice of pants, not just from the hype that had so effectively made it popular in the end, but because the jeans themselves would be made from super high-quality materials, and that was what was going to keep us at the height of our success for many years to come.

When we got in our first shipment of five thousand jeans, we started to give them to my friends who were celebrities and then to stylists. At that point, it was make it or break it, literally. It was a gamble. A big gamble.

> **You get what you pay for**

I was out doing guerrilla marketing. I kept the jeans in the car and would sell them anywhere I stopped. I was like a dealer.

I saw this cute guy, Rich Lazenby, now a partner at the law firm Condon & Forsyth, who is still my friend to this day. He loves to tell the story of how he was shopping at Bristol Farms in Manhattan Beach and this crazy girl ran up to him with braids and a big smile, telling him, "I would like to give you a pair of jeans to wear."

I knew people would notice him, he was sexy. He was just the type I wanted to market my jean.

I started giving the pants to stores on consignment. People said "No" to True Religion for a year. Here we had made these five thousand units and now they were just sitting in a warehouse. We had stayed true to our conviction in making the jeans, now we just had to sell them!

Five Thousand Jeans and Nowhere to Go

We knew we needed to get the jeans known. Sales were in a tailspin. The stores we had given the pants to on consignment had customers returning the pants. The men's jean pockets were bigger, with a twisted seam, not a basic five pocket. People just didn't get it. The smaller stores would tell us the customers didn't like them and that they didn't sell well. So a lot of those stores returned their inventory back to us. But we were steadfast in waiting for the "Yes."

Our first set of reps was not as aggressive as we needed them to be. Normally, when a store writes an order from a rep in a showroom, the store's buyer signs a purchase order, then the clothing company ships out the product. There has to be a real legitimate reason to return something. True Religion was so new and innovative that our sales team, who didn't have knowledge of our particular category of clothing, didn't understand how to sell our jeans.

It would have behooved our sales rep to say to the buyers, "These are new, give it another week."

The sales reps don't get paid if the stores return the jeans.

Every day during that period, I would take a breath, suit up, show up, and just focus on marching forward. And "No" was not an option. It had to become a "Yes." It just had to. There were times when I thought, "Fuck this. I'll go become a designer for someone else again." But then I would just carry on to the next moment, hand out another pair of jeans, and let that thought pass. It had to work. I needed it—for me, for us, for the family. It was like I willed it to be.

There's no doubt it was a challenge. There were big stores that said "No" for years. Neiman Marcus said "No." They were the ones who wanted us to change the logo, get rid of the Buddha, and change the name. Everything about it was "No, no, no," and we didn't change any of it. Ultimately, Neiman Marcus carried the line. It was like Sylvester Stallone wanting to be in his own movie. I was in my own movie. This was my movie. This was my vision, and I was not willing to give it up.

We had given Fred Segal several pairs to sell in their Santa Monica store in their Fun Department. When I came back two weeks later, not one pair had been sold. My heart dropped. People thought they looked strange with the pocket so low and the look of the stitching. So I gave the salesperson a pair to try on. She loved them and never wore another jean. She was our best advertising. After seeing them on her, shoppers would inquire, and suddenly we had the jeans selling out at Fred Segal. They would be gone every time I went back to see if they needed another order. Some of it was just timing and luck. After a year of hearing "No," we were *finally* starting to hear a peppering of "Yes," and then the momentum kicked in. It was the weirdest thing. This was before social media, so there wasn't the ability to get the word out in a tweet. This was grassroots. People had to have the Joey.

The jeans hit their stride in Japan before the trend struck in the US. The Japanese market came through our manufacturer in Gardena, Tony Shibata. He was a Japanese distributor. Oftentimes designers get those buyer relationships through trade shows, or New York reps when buyers from Asia come to the markets to see what's new and hot. The Japanese love American brands; they saw True Religion and bought them in bulk. Both the men's and women's, which we had just started to roll out. Getting the Japanese orders was the easy part.

It's a whole separate size scale for the Asian market. For Americans, the sizes run from twenty-four inches to thirty-one, with the bulk of production focusing in the middle sizes, ranging between twenty-five inches and twenty-eight inches. In Japan, you only make sizes ranging from twenty-two inches to twenty-eight inches. You rarely make twenty-eights. So you have to really focus on a whole other sizing scale.

Once it caught on here in the United States, when True Religion finally became the jeans to have, they were on fire!

Then girls started wearing the men's jeans. I knew there could be a boyfriend jean, meaning a man's jean that women could wear. The Joey was cute and baggy, it was non-stretch, and women could wear them and look sexy. Girls really loved them, which just added to our market share.

Scoop, one of the well-known designer boutiques in New York, and more recently Los Angeles, had a buyer who was a real bitch to us in the beginning. Our sales rep had sold a large order of the jeans to her. After the buyer bought them, she felt the pockets were too big, so she returned them, all of them. She returned everything. Then, when the jeans took off, she came back to my rep and wanted to carry them. I was emphatic.

"No! I'm sorry they didn't do well for you and you didn't want them. Now that you see everyone else can't keep them on the shelves, now you want them. No!"

I hate that. I really do. And luckily for us at the time, we were doing well enough with so many other stores that I could take that stance and stick to it.

People are not willing to line up to be first; instead they want to be first to be second. I believe we should take chances on something new, not buy the same thing. Stores don't take a chance on new designs anymore. Stores should partner with designers. If everything gets returned by the retailer, and they won't support the designer, how can a forward-thinking designer stay in business? So often retailers are on to the next, and so often the "next" is a rehash of what is already out there. There's no loyalty.

I had more than four companies before True Religion. I had sketches in my portfolio of the precursor to the Joey jean I had done for other designers that never got picked up. Fashion is about timing, and with True Religion it was the right style, at the right time, for the right amount of money.

One of my good friends, Lisa Kline, had one of the best boutiques on Robertson. She says even to this day, "I fucked up. I should have bought it."

Before we became a phenomenon, Lisa wasn't sure. "I know your other brands did well, but it's not for me."

Because she didn't buy them, I had to sell it across the street to another store, Kitson. Once we became a sensation, I couldn't sell it to Lisa, because Kitson was across the street. Lisa had to watch as Kitson did phenomenal numbers with our clothes. Lisa wished she had been first, that's for sure.

My sewing contractor would give me the damages for nothing, which was so helpful. Often, if a clothing company has damages, the manufacturer sells them off to jobbers downtown to repurpose, which is what I had done when I'd sold T-shirts in Venice. Those damaged jeans were a huge opportunity in my mind. They had a slight flaw, maybe the pockets were off a little bit, the wash wasn't up to standard, or whatever the reason was that we couldn't charge the full two hundred fifty dollars and up that the jeans were going for in stores. I realized it was better to keep the slightly flawed jeans and give them as a "Thank you" to the many who had helped in some way. It was the perfect offering of goodwill. The many friends, family, and business associates I had would be delighted to get a pair of True Religions as a gift, and it wouldn't affect our bottom line.

It can be an expensive acquisition if you give away product, but it's an underground guerrilla marketing tactic that

I still believe in wholeheartedly that engages your friends, their friends, and ultimately your sales. By giving your friends your product, you are partnering with them, getting your people to start having a conversation. Clothes are a great way to engage for a girl—"I like your shoes." Or your bag, or whatever it is.

When you see your friend tell her friend, or boyfriend, and then his friend, and that other guy, it becomes a subliminal advertising campaign.

We got really lucky. Our tenacity paid off, and True Religion expanded beyond our wildest dreams. Actually, it wasn't beyond what I could have imagined—it was what I had dreamed of all along.

Six

RE-ORDER

Three out of five. That is the number of people I counted wearing True Religion jeans while I was walking down the street in a concentrated area of boutiques in Manhattan Beach in the blazing summer of 2005. Three out of five!

After seeing our explosive success, our dear friend, Gary, introduced us to a group of investors who wanted to come on board to get the company in a position to go public. They gave us money to expand, which we used to build our brand and organize our company. It was time to start offering shares. We started as a penny stock.

Everywhere I looked, both men and women were wearing our premier jean—our only jean at that point, called the Joey, which Jeff had named after a cousin. What a thrill to see almost every tush that slid in front of me had that signature pocket with the twisted seam and button flap. It was an extraordinary feeling to have "arrived."

After all we had been through, the struggles and fear of believing in something so absolutely that we put everything we had into it, both financially as well as emotionally, while waiting for others to see it, too. It was a euphoric feeling when the public finally responded, and in a monumental way.

I imagine it similar to a band who has their first breakout hit on the radio, and everyone thinks they're brand-new, only to realize it took them ten years of touring before their song shot to number one. That was my situation with True Religion. I had been sixteen years in the industry, creating the brand, all while having children before we created something that was beyond what we could even fathom.

I'm not saying it takes that long necessarily; it could be less or more. My process was long and arduous. And we were an anomaly. It doesn't always happen where you build a brand, go public, and get a payoff.

We were definitely not an overnight success. But, in creating the Joey, we were now a household name . . . we were True Religion.

I had struggled, worked, begged, borrowed, and, well, everything *but* stolen, to make these jeans and the company a reality. And now, according to our sales numbers, they would be on three out of five people throughout the world. It was a miracle! I hold my emotions close and I'm not a crier, but at that moment, on that day, really acknowledging the phenomenon, I could feel the tears welling up. If I had let myself, I could have sobbed.

With all the years I had put in as a designer, it was cathartic to finally see the fruition of all the hard work I had done on all the previous lines I had created, culminating into the success of this, *my* company.

I had struggled to start True Religion in 2002 with Jeff, and now here I was, only three years later, and it was a very different experience.

It Was Magic

It was Magic Market Week in Las Vegas, where buyers for retail clothing stores come from all over the world to shop for their next season. All the hip companies, from Seven Jeans, Levi, Paul Smith, up and coming James Perse, and now True Religion, had booths to show their lines of clothing, footwear, and miscellaneous accessories for the upcoming season.

I walked through the entrance doors of the convention center with our Japanese distributor, Tony Shibata. On the floor, buyers, designers, and fashionistas buzzed around the various booths chatting with the clothing reps and designers of the various new lines. A DJ was scratching albums on a podium, so the music had a pounding dance beat, while models paraded provocatively around wearing a designer's latest statement.

As we shuffled our way through the masses toward the True Religion booth, I noticed there was this big frenzy of buyers waiting in a long line that wrapped around the corner.

Generally, buyers won't wait for any length of time to spend their allocated dollars for that season. They'll come back to that designer later, when they can be fawned over and serviced quickly. So I thought it was odd that they were all just standing in anxious anticipation. I said to Tony, "That can't be our booth." The possibility was too abstract to even fathom.

As we turned the corner, Tony smiled and pointed, "I think it is your booth."

I looked in disbelief.

"Are you fucking kidding me? It can't be!" It was our booth. I was giggly with delight.

There was a competitive line of people snaked in the direction of our showroom. We had an amazing sales rep, Jana, who gave our trade show booth the feeling of Studio 54. It was an incredible space that echoed the underground cool of the jean.

Your sales reps are one of the most important parts of the business. They should be someone who knows the garment as well as the designer and can communicate to the retailer why they have to have the pant. The more enthusiasm they have, the better, and it is just as important that they can be strategic in placing the product in stores. You don't want to be a Starbucks on every block. You want to be in that one store on that block. It's the missing puzzle in your business. That rep can make or break you.

Every buyer at the show that year wanted True Religion jeans in their stores, and they wanted them *bad*.

There was a celebrity element to that moment of success, where I just thought, "Oh my god, really? It happened?!" It's the Sally Field's Oscar moment of, "They like me, they really like me!" I felt elated by the whole experience and suddenly it almost made it all worth it. All the stress, all the work, and the time away from the kids, it all meant something. I couldn't wait to call Jeff and tell him the good news.

Take time to cherish your successes

I took a second to bask in the moment. It was like I'd been holding my shoulders taut from a constant state of anxiety for the last couple of years and now I could finally let them relax and drop down. It felt *so* good!

Arriving at the booth, it was as though I was having an out of body experience as I started shaking hands with the effusive buyers who were so complimentary about the line.

It was overwhelming in its intensity, and I didn't miss the irony in being heralded by the very people who were so hard to contact in the beginning. Our popularity was undeniable. We were basking in the momentum and ready to utilize the public's fervor for our jeans to grow the company. Finally, after all I had been through, they had come to buy my merchandise. And they bought a lot.

How Am I Going to Do It?

I took a moment to absorb the reality that the jeans were a hit with the consumers, being bought by buyers, and the respect I was getting from my peers. That is a winning trifecta in the garment industry. That moment of euphoria, however, is fleeting. God forbid such a feeling of joy should stay with me for any length of time. My bliss was suddenly clouded with, *Oh my god, oh my god, oh my god! How am I going to do it?!*

There were so many orders that I had no idea how I was going to get all those clothes made by the delivery dates. But, I knew one thing: I would *fucking* find a way.

The definition of the word "phenomenon" in the dictionary reads, "someone or something that is very impressive or popular especially because of an unusual ability or quality." That was us! True Religion had become the very definition of a phenomenon.

When I got back to Los Angeles, JLo's and Beyoncé's stylists came to me and asked for jeans for events and photo shoots. I was more than happy to personally deliver the jeans to their houses at any time of the day or night. I was still living in my grassroots mentality of, "I will do anything to get the jeans anywhere!" The press we got from those artists wearing our clothes was priceless.

It was the beginning of the era where stylists were making a statement for their clients in everything they wore. It used to be that there would be the occasional mention of what a celeb was wearing in some fashion magazine, the Academy Awards, and the "Worked" and "Didn't" photos comparing two notable people wearing the same designer outfit in *People* magazine. But, generally, actors and singers didn't have *every* outfit completely "crafted" by a stylist as they do today, with every item of clothing and designer being rattled off at every event and red carpet appearance.

The first celebrity to wear our premier pant, the Joey, was one of my best friends since junior high school, Holly Robinson Peete. She wore those jeans anywhere and everywhere she thought they might be noticed or photographed. She was quickly followed by interest from Usher, Halle Berry, Eric Benét, and Beyoncé. Stylists would call and say, "I have to get your jeans for my client, they want them *now!*"

Again, I would jump into my Range Rover (which I could finally afford) and schlep to wherever was necessary to drop off a goody bag of jeans. The next week there would be a photo in *Us* or *People* of that celebrity wearing the Joey at some movie premiere or event around town.

The night of the GRAMMY's, at his request, I dropped off several pairs to Usher at his hotel. He wore the Joey during his performance on the show with the world watching him. That next week, our sales numbers rose exponentially again.

In November of that year, our company made its way into music history. Not on stage, but in song. I came home to emails and messages from different friends, family, and business associates. Each message was stranger than the next:

"Have you listened to 'My Humps' yet?! You've got listen to it! I don't want to ruin it." *Click.*

"You are not going to *believe* what Fergie said!" *Click.*

"You need to turn on VH1 or MTV *right* now!" *Click.*

The Black Eyed Peas were one of the hottest bands out at that moment, and the song "My Humps" had shot up to the top ten on Billboard's Hot 100 list. It stayed there for six weeks.

When I finally did hear the song, I couldn't miss it. No one could. Fergie rapped:

"Brother I ain't askin,
They say they love my ass 'n,
Seven Jeans, True Religion's,
I say no, but they keep givin'"

There it was . . . Fergie talking about wearing True Religion jeans. That mention in her song catapulted our popularity yet again. We had become solidified as a hip underground sensation. The truth of it is, it took weeks before I could even get a minute to take the time to listen to the song; everything was spinning so fast there wasn't an extra second in the day to do anything but make sure the kids were alive and fed. True Religion was holding steady (if not gaining), and we had to get started on the next project to ensure the company's success.

Our clients were clamoring even more for the Joey jeans. We were ready to get our orders out to our vendors for our new Women's Twisted Seamed Joey Stretch. We couldn't get them sewn quick enough. We were so new to the manufacturing company making the jeans for us, they just didn't take us seriously. We were a start-up, they didn't see any back orders, they just saw us with this one order.

Manufacturers are an assembly line—they have a line of machines, with payroll and staff, but if there wasn't a back-up order from the designer then they look at it and say, "Okay, it's five thousand jeans, but there's not another order for more coming. So this may be it."

When we got our order of thousands of pants in every size, every one had come out wrong. The pockets were off, which was the biggest issue for me, and one leg was longer than the other in some. We were using a stretch material, which was new to manufacturers who didn't have a handle on how to sew the material evenly yet. I was hysterical, shouting on the phone to the owner that they'd ruined us! He thought I was a screaming PMS maniac, which just annoyed me more. Anyone would have reacted as I had. He offered a discount to appease me. I bellowed. "I don't want a discount! I want my goods right!"

For someone who is a perfectionist and detail-oriented, this was the type of situation that could get me in a padded cell. There was nothing anyone could do.

There are always issues in production. We were at the site all the time. This was the first round of production, so we could certainly fix the problem for the next round and obviously talk face to face with the pattern makers, cutters for fabric, and (when calmer heads prevailed) the head of production, to discuss the sewing machines for the next order. It's all very tedious, and these pants were very difficult to sew.

But unless I wanted to wait the month or so it would take to get the replacements, I had to have faith that the pants were good enough and that no one would notice.

The orders were already two months late, which was incredibly anxiety provoking. If we had sent them all back . . . well, it just wasn't an option. We just had to go with it and move forward. With all the buzz around us, the timeliness of getting the women's pants into the stores was imperative. We didn't have any choice but to ship out the order. I could barely sleep, anxious that the stores would return everything and we would have to replace it all. We shipped out all the orders and I waited by the phone, ready to have to defend our decision to our retailers. Instead, to my relief and amusement, every store sold out their inventory within the first week. Instead of calling to complain, they ordered more!

As grateful as I was that we had slid under the radar, I was extremely "vocal" to our manufacturer that his incompetence had better never happen again. He got the message, and our next order was executed perfectly.

For me, part of the thrill of the new women's jean being such a success was that I had been the fit model. I was a curvy girl. I had three kids who were all under the age of seven. I was fit, but had a bit of a tush and hips. I felt we were an underserved demographic. The skinny jeans other companies made were sized to fit a stick insect. My goal was to fit girls like me—J Lo, Beyoncé, and other women with curves. "Healthy" women at that point were singled out in not having size options. People would always say to me, "They fit my tush!" True Religion was a jean they could wear.

There are a much larger percentage of women with curvy bodies than there are the skinny minnies living in New York and Los Angeles. And I was there to service that portion of the population.

It was kind of sad to me that I had actually always wanted to be uber thin growing up. I had a strong, fantastically fit body in my teens and completely under-appreciated it. Instead, I compared myself to six-foot models I would never be, no matter how little I ate. It had always been a constant argument with myself throughout life.

Needless to say, I found wry humor in the fact that because of my voluptuous body type, I was basically making the women's jean for myself. And yet it was that fit that became the allure of the jean. At that point, I didn't necessarily have a plan in mind, I just couldn't find any jean that fit my body. It was pure serendipity that we were the first company out in the market offering a more curvy style in a trendy jean.

Be first

That year, I went to a GRAMMY after-party with Holly, thrown by a massive entrepreneur, Ronald Burkle, who had one every year. It was attended by every top celebrity known to man, all of who had been at the awards earlier that evening. When I arrived, I veered over to get a drink and suddenly Holly came rushing over.

"They all want to meet you!" she cried.

Holly knows everyone. She's been in the industry since she was a kid. Her big break was starring on *21 Jump Street* before going on to become an entertainment mogul. Everybody in entertainment was friends with her. Holly grabbed my drink and used it as a carrot to beckon me over to a crowd including Eve and En Vogue, announcing, "This is my friend Kym, the one who owns True Religion."

I cringed at the introduction, but everyone gushed about the pants and soon I was absorbed into their conversations, as though I was one of the gang.

A week or so later, I was at the office and the phone rang. It was early and the receptionist we had finally hired wasn't in yet. I picked up and a voice said, "Hi, this is Tommy Hilfiger. I'm looking for Kym or Jeff."

I said the obvious, "Get the fuck out of here." And promptly hung up.

Prank callers. A moment later, the phone rang again. It was really him. Once I could get my heart to stop pulsating through my head long enough to hear what Tommy was saying, I was able to make out that he wanted to meet at the Four Seasons in Beverly Hills to discuss working together on a clothing line.

We were over our heads already with orders and to even think of doing more was crazy, but it was Tommy Hilfiger! And it wasn't just him; we had pro basketball players wanting to do a jean, Aerosmith had a T-shirt idea, Randy Jackson had something he wanted to do. Our phone was constantly ringing with new opportunities. Every minute of every day was spoken for in figuring out how to make sure we didn't drop the ball. It was a constant barrage of questions and needs from all quadrants of our lives. We were so inundated, we didn't have time to enjoy the moment, we just focused on what was next in the day.

The Red Carpet

It was almost like I was becoming a celebrity myself because I was around so many of them. I would walk into parties and there would be Jessica Alba, and Lil' Kim mingling with Eve, and waving at me as I made my way to the bar. It was very surreal. I was getting invited to the *GRAMMY's*, *BET Awards*, fashion parties, and Jimmy Choo events.

So much success was happening almost simultaneously that I didn't ever have time to really wallow in it. I just rode the wave, making sure to stay on. It was time to open the first retail store. The obvious location was Manhattan Beach, because that was home.

After designing the store, I organized the opening party. Even I couldn't believe what a hit it was. It was packed with stylists, celebrities, editors, journalists, big hitters in the fashion culture that could make or break a designer. We couldn't move inside, and each person I bumped into I recognized from the fashion world. At that time it was not a situation of buying ad space to get editorials. The editors and journalists had full reign over the direction and conversation of the fashion evolution, and they were all advocates for True Religion.

From the moment we opened the doors of the Manhattan Beach store, we couldn't keep enough inventory in it. I took on the responsibility of opening the other upcoming retail locations.

Just before I started the next round of stores, I went to Tokyo with Michelle. It was right after I had opened Manhattan Beach. I felt an immediate camaraderie with the Japanese sales associates when I saw the way they took such pride in their boutiques. From the gift-wrapping to their display of merchandise, it was pristine, it was precise, and it was classy. It was everything I had intended for my stores.

Japan's sense of grace was so far above what we had in the States. From top designers like Ralph Lauren to the more moderate stores such as Levi's, every one of them in Tokyo had an incredible eye for detail, all of which was so attractive to me. They also had a full-service attitude. Again, a way of working that fully resonated with me.

In each of the True Religion stores I visited in Tokyo, the personnel knew who I was and treated me as though it was a red carpet event to have me there. I was honored and impressed with their generosity.

I came back wanting to emulate that same sense of honor in retail. I had always wanted to be the Nordstrom's of customer service. I would often wonder why in America I would walk into stores and the sales people would be bitchy, going, "And you're here because . . .?" I hate that. I'm sorry, isn't this where you buy things?

Right after I got back from Japan, I opened up four more stores: Miami; New York on Prince Street; Los Angeles on Robertson; and an outlet store in Cabazon.

Opening day at the Cabazon store, I arrived in the morning to find people had already started to line up to be the first in to buy. It was like they were waiting for a concert. I looked out the window at the planted hipsters waiting to get in and really felt like we had street cred. It was such a great feeling to be in the mix with the actual public all waiting to own a pair of True Religion jeans.

Seven

THE FITTING

A reverse merger, also known as reverse IPO, is what happened with True Religion. It's where a private company acquires the majority of the shares of a public company and they merge. Usually the public company is defunct and simply a publicly traded shell. It is a relatively simple and inexpensive way to "go public." This allows for more liquidity and access to capital markets while also creating more strategic options to pursue growth, such as acquisitions using the stock as currency.

I had never been a part of a public company before. Having done it, I don't think it needs to be a goal for a business. It all depends on what you need.

Before you can think about whether or not to go public, you need to start with your plan and setting goals for your business. There is so much to starting up a company that is of utmost importance to prepare for how you can successfully move forward: writing a business plan and mission statement; figuring out who your demographic is; figuring out how many pieces you want to make—are you doing dresses, bottoms, tops? How many fabrics of each style; how many reps will you need; what part of the country are you going to sell in; will you develop an in-house line for a store; do you need to create lookbooks; how many bodies in the line; and what is your price point?

Just to get to a trade show, there are a multitude of travel expenses. You can spend half a million dollars before you know it on just the lookbooks you create and the samples you take to the show. You need a sample line for your New York reps and LA reps, and perhaps another offset line for on the road; a minimum of five lines per season to start off.

If you go smaller, you can get by on one rep. If you only attend one show twice a year, my suggestion would be the Coterie show. To have one rep, you will essentially pay rent for their showroom. In that case, you become the landlord of that showroom. You pay for the building, the staff, and getting the samples to your reps to sell.

Say a garment costs twenty dollars to make in bulk. To get one garment made as a sample, it's two and a half times the price it would be at the bulk rate. It's an expensive venture to start off on, and if you don't know your fabric and it shrinks, you could lose your shirt. No pun intended.

Then there is the question of quantities to order. If you sell one hundred units at the Coterie show, do you want to make 10 or 15 percent over the hundred pieces you are going to have manufactured? If you do, then you have pieces to give away to editors, friends, and reorder business.

Of course the scale of money will depend on your fabric, your rent, if you are working out of your home, printing your own lookbook, and will only have an online presence. There's certainly more ways of doing it now, but you have to do your research before going in.

Those are only the big issues that will come up before getting you to the place of asking the question, "Do I want to go public?"

I wouldn't do it again. I'm completely grateful I had that experience, but I wouldn't do it that way again. Going public was a process. We were given two hundred and fifty thousand dollars and our majority shares in True Religion by a company that wanted to roll True Religion into a public shell. The introduction was through dear friends we had vacationed with on our honeymoon those many years ago in Hawaii.

In 2004, we started selling shares starting at sixty-five cents over the counter and then gradually the price got higher. Because our jeans were so popular by that time, the stock catapulted straight up along with them. A company can't go on the NASDAQ until it hits seven dollars a share. We never had to advertise—from the underground swell of buyers we hit the seven-dollar mark in just over two years. Jeff would say, "We're worth fifteen million dollars on paper!"

That made me nervous, I would try to impress upon him that paper doesn't mean anything.

The investor site Benzinga stated, "True Religion may be the only example of a penny stock scheme-turned successful company in the history of the stock market." We had made it to the NASDAQ.

The Boardroom

Fight to get women on your board of directors

When the company went public, we interviewed people and started to accumulate our board of directors. We found a well-entrenched group of guys, all of who came from substantial companies in various aspects of the clothing and retail industries. I had pushed for a couple of women, but Jeff, being CEO, had the deciding voice. And I didn't know enough about it to know I should hold steadfast to my request.

The board is really there for the shareholders, to make sure their stock is making money. For me, having gone public, it became more arduous and less glamorous, and there was much more time spent on that aspect of the business rather than designing clothes.

Because we were on the NASDAQ, we had a lot more visibility. And, as a public company, we were spending so much more time dealing with it. There was a litany of protocol I had to learn, including how long I had to hold on to my stocks before I could sell!

I was constantly having to take classes and seminars. They brought people in to explain the issues of sexual harassment; audits; what I could and couldn't write on my computer; what I could and could not say about having a public company. I couldn't say shit about anything! I could say, "We're public and doing well." Period. I couldn't give specifics.

My family never bought shares of the penny stock when they could, for whatever reason. They could have, but I guess they didn't believe in it enough to invest. Because of the company's success, those shares became an issue that would become a fight later in life when a certain member felt entitled to them. As much as we were so excited and wanted to share the specifics and details of the innards of the public area of our company, we just couldn't.

You have to have minutes of each board of directors meeting, and all of that takes away from the creative process. When you have a public company, it isn't yours anymore; it's the village's company. They all put money in and want to tell you what you can and cannot do.

We had to have board of directors meetings on a regular basis. I wanted to do limited editions of clothing items for the stores. My idea was that if the item was limited, we could charge more. Finally, the board let me try it.

I took all the damaged clothes from the manufacturers and deconstructed each piece and re-sewed it, or embroidered on it, or put on patches. The clothes became one-of-a-kind and although they cost more to make, we charged more for it being a "limited" item. In the end the board didn't see it as advantageous for the shareholders, even though the margins were exponentially larger.

I believed it was those nuances to the clothes that made True Religion special, but I had to fight for that one. I wanted to continue, but the board and Jeff saw more financial gain in doing regular lines of other styles. I had to choose my battles.

I was dealing with a whole new set of circumstances with a public company. I had so many new responsibilities. Among them, to learn how a public company worked, and learn the SEC laws and other important legalities.

Martha Stewart had just been imprisoned for securities fraud, among other allegations. I was glued to the verdict as the prosecutor had to hold back tears of joy.

The enormity of my culpability lay heavy on my mind as I spoke in the meetings. It changed my perception on how much to say about anything, for fear I could end up imprisoned for not knowing the laws.

There was an intense pressure and stress on me to prepare presentations, sell enough, and meet the general expectations of the board. I would have liked the opportunity to talk with the shareholders, but that was never an option.

After I was on the board for a couple of months, the guys all got comfortable with having me there and soon they began putting their proverbial dicks on the table to see whose was the biggest. I would say, "Really guys? We're talking about T-shirts."

And God forbid I would say anything about their macho behavior—I was considered a bitch.

I was becoming aggressive about where the designs should go in our meetings. Jeff was adamant about not advertising, the board wanted to advertise, and I liked the hands-on approach. I think advertising is always important, but I liked the growth at the rate we were growing it. We were reaching out to a lot more consumers and creating a long-standing relationship in selling our way.

On our board, some of the men knew business and some came from capital interests, and some were older than the hills. Being the only woman, the youngest, outspoken, and considered a bitch, I was defensive. Then Jeff and I would argue.

He knew about fabric, but he hadn't been on my end, out there with the sales reps going to shows, designing, and being part of the process. Being in the trenches, I think I knew what the zeitgeist was in the country, if not the world. I wasn't thinking, "These are the board members and I have shareholders I have to appease." I thought, "I want to make the best product and get it out there."

In working with all men in this capacity, it led me to understand that, if allowed, they lead with their dicks in everything they do. Everything is based on their egos. As the only woman dealing with the male-dominant force in the room, it was hard to be taken seriously. I would often wish there were more women in the room to balance it out. I became almost a nuisance, a bit like I was the conscience that they didn't want to reconcile with—so by my being there they had to keep some semblance of decorum going in the meeting. It was as though I was their moral compass, which they didn't want to listen to, but knew was there.

There were those pleasantries that happen in the beginning of a meeting, as not everyone was there in person. Some were on the phone. The moment we were ready to talk about business, there would be a quiet in the room as the board waited to see how Jeff and I were doing as a couple.

Jeff would talk about the quarterly and fiscal reporting. I always felt like I wasn't heard. If I tried to mention something to do with the information he was presenting, Jeff would say, "Okay, Kym, thanks," as though it wasn't important.

Jeff would take control of the meeting and I wouldn't have any input. It became like the *War of the Roses*.

One day I said, "Listen, we're doing the same washes and stretch, let me do a cute dress or a blazer."

The clothing line needed to expand. Michael Buckley, our COO, and I would have many discussions. We would try to expand, and Jeff would veto. As vice president of Women's, my responsibility was to do other things: a holiday line, cute blazers, fun T-shirts.

Even though you are a denim company, you need to give your consumers something else to buy. They'll buy three T-shirts to one pair of jeans, or grab a cute blazer to finish the look.

I ended up doing cute blazers. I was able to procure great accessories and shoes for the company. I found vintage belts through a vendor in LA, and a woman who hand-crocheted scarves that could be sent off as a prototype to make en masse. I made parka vests and we expanded into corduroy jeans, which was fine with the board because they were familiar with it being a jean. I offered really great colors for spring. I was given a little rope, but not enough.

At the time, Zihad, one of the design directors, would have to stand witness to Jeff and my arguments. It was difficult for him. He could see both my side and Jeff's side, but Jeff and I had a marriage that was having problems as well. It created an animosity between the women's department and the men's department.

The Bedroom

I knew Jeff loved me, but our relationship had become a difficult one. It felt arduous at the best of times. I didn't want to put our boys through a divorce. Each time we considered separating, we would find a comfortable middle ground emotionally and live together for a while longer until the tide changed. But this time was different.

The situation pushed the employees to form camps. There was the Kym side and the Jeff side. More and more often, employees were privy to disagreements in design meetings. The board members were in Jeff's corner. They were upset every time I complained about the business, which was not being run well.

At one point, Steven Tyler came to the office and wanted his own line. We couldn't even get our own T-shirts made properly, and they wanted to do Aerosmith's line. I voiced that and, needless to say, they were not happy with my remarks.

I didn't then, and still don't see the relevance in the building of a new company based on a celebrity. To bring in and spend the money on a line for Steven—I didn't see how that could elevate our brand at the time. I could see a celebrity promoting the brand by wearing the clothes, but spending money for a Steven Tyler line didn't make sense to me. We were still trying to build our brand internationally. It became a point of contention, especially as it was me saying it. Although they did step away from doing Steven's line, it was on the board's terms.

For Jeff's fiftieth birthday, we celebrated at the office. I had spent a year collecting vinyl I knew he liked: Janice

Joplin, Grateful Dead, and Hot Tuna (who mentioned True Religion in their music), along with a new record player. I was so excited to present it to him. The anticipation was killing me, so when he opened it up and there was no reaction, I was crushed. Outwardly, it seemed as though it meant nothing to him. Of course he still has it, but he didn't acknowledge it then, which gutted me. We were past the point of no return. It went both ways.

Jeff started flying private planes to Vegas for the Magic Trade Show. The meetings were becoming more and more an old boys' club. I was watching as these guys became more arrogant with every dollar made. It was a recipe for disaster.

One of the shareholders had a dinner. We discussed some philanthropic ideas. I like to get involved with charities. I feel lucky and am grateful in having the money and opportunity I have and feel compelled to pay it forward.

That night, we talked of creating a charity and giving one percent of our profits to it. Jeff vetoed it immediately. I was furious that my request was simply cast aside. I would have fought harder, but it was embarrassing. It was a constant fight for a conscientious equilibrium at the company. I always had to be strategic with my ideas, otherwise they would be shot down.

I was bored by it all and didn't want to be there. I had become a quick study in learning all the rules and regulations of being a public company, but there was still more information on the FCC (Federal Communications Commission) I needed to learn and other nuances to being on the board. It was like a whole other job.

Eventually, I'm sure I seemed completely disinterested. I wanted to design, and instead I was reading legal mandates on tariff rates. Then, when I did design a piece, Jeff would veto it. I would design something else, and it would get refused as well. It was an ongoing tug of war.

The worst part of it was that I was so busy that the boys were feeling neglected. Of course they knew I loved them, but our time together was compromised with every new line released and new store opened. There just weren't enough hours in the day.

One of many stings to follow happened on May 4, 2006, at 6:30 a.m. I knew Jeff had gone to New York for a meeting. I was at home getting the boys ready for school. When I arrived into work, there was an obvious excitement in the air, and as I walked through the office I received a few congratulatory pats on the back and praise such as "Big day!" and "Wasn't Jeff great!" from various employees. I could feel my heart beginning to race. The strength it took for me to not react was Herculean.

Jeff had rung the bell that morning at 9:30 a.m. at the NASDAQ Marketsite in Times Square, New York, to commemorate True Religion's listing. And I knew nothing about it. I had not been invited.

The moment I was alone, I called Jeff. "What the fuck? You didn't think to mention this to me? You didn't think I might like to join you on this auspicious day? You didn't think I might like to at least be *mentioned* specifically as the co-creator, rather than the anemic quote you offered?"

"What's the big deal? We never travel together!" Jeff exclaimed. "I didn't think it was a big deal for you." He didn't see an issue. "After all, I am the CEO," he finally said.

The quote went like this: "We are honored to participate in the NASDAQ opening bell ceremony. This is a great privilege for our company and I would like to recognize the hard work and commitment of our employees who made our NASDAQ listing possible. We are very focused on expanding the presence of the True Religion Apparel brand both in the US and abroad and believe that ringing the opening bell is a gratifying way to reward our success."

The business was being ripped out from under me. There were all too many interviews and magazine covers of which only Jeff had been the focus, telling the reporters how it was all *his* hard work that started True Religion and the occasional mention of my name in tandem with "employee" or "wife," giving a strong impression that he was doing me a favor by giving me a job in 2004 (as written in many postings) rather than the truth. He had always said that if we weren't going to be together, I wasn't going to be working at the company. I knew he planned to honor his promise.

Many people knew what was about to happen. Jeff is a tyrant, so to fight against him, I became one. It's as though I was fighting to protect my child.

I was defiant . . . but not only in my stance against Jeff. I was asked quite a few times after a board meeting why Jeff was slurring and couldn't hear. These people would coward down to him and yet come to me to ask about him. My reply would be, "Ask him yourself! Why are you coming to me with that question?" It became like a Shakespearean play.

I was being treated as Jeff's wife rather than getting the respect I deserved.

I knew denim was a staple, but it was important to expand to sweatpants, knit pants, and other styles. Neiman Marcus had wanted us to give them an idea for a dress they might offer. Jeff kept saying we were a denim business, not a dress business. I fought him on it and wanted to give them a design. I created a light chambray (lightweight denim) halter dress that I was really proud of, but the pushback was huge. I was on the brink of giving up the fight to offer up the dress, but at the last minute pulled out the sample at a meeting with the buyer. As it turned out, it came out in the Neiman's catalog, a huge feat for any designer. I felt incredibly vindicated by that.

And yet, when Jeff decided we should do a French Terry jean, mocking our five-pocket Joey, it was a disaster because of the construction in using the same stitching process as a regular jean material. Jeff accused me of wanting the construction for the women's, but I hadn't wanted it—he was just trying to make me the scapegoat. So we fought.

I wanted sexy for the women's line; he wanted tomboy. He didn't want African Americans in the ads; I did. I chose lookbooks that looked similar to what Benetton is now—we were an international brand!

People around the office had issue that I wasn't in a good mood, or being nice every day. How could I be? My marriage and life were falling apart. Somebody was taking my baby away from me. With Bella Dahl having been stolen, the endless people who took advantage of us, and losing all our money, it was long-suffering and excruciating to constantly have to suit up for battle every day.

Around the office, I was like a walking protester, because I was championing something I had built and cared about. Who in their right mind would assume I would say, "Okay, bye-bye"? No damn way. So, of course, I made enemies during the demise of my position in the company.

The Plan

Something had to give. Jeff had always threatened that if I left him, he would take the company from me. The more confident he became in knowing he would maintain his hold on the business, the more the wheels were put into motion. He could see the growth of the company and what that meant with the amount of my shares. The board would ask him, "What are you going to do, Jeff?"

The board members may have said they would give him more shares if I were gone. They didn't listen to me anyway, and they all believed Jeff's story. But there was no way for him to feel confident enough to do what he did without having something in place for himself, that took place behind the scenes. Jeff's a smart guy.

It became clearer by the day that the public would never have any idea that I had any involvement in creating the brand. I had given the company as much importance as my children in order to get it up and running—which, as a mother, still causes a pang of guilt every day—and no one would ever know it.

I wanted a divorce.

The award winning faces of *Faces International.*
Michelle, Traci, me

It's all about the details. True Religion charity event.
Babyface Edmonds, Holly Robinson Peete, me

My handsome sons.
Dylan, Jake, Ryan.

The beginning of an empire.
Me, Jeff

Before *Survivor*, there was just us.
Mark Burnett, me

Where there is good music, there is RJ.
Me, Randy Jackson

Pink (Alecia) and the girls.
Me, Pink, Michelle, Traci

We're not acting . . . we're in love.
Marlon Young, me

The designer at work.

My true BFF.
Holly Robinson Peete, me

The original Joey jeans.

Selling clothes in Venice back in the day.

Selling in Venice, so much to do, so little time.

Bat mitzvah in triplicate.

Family fun.
Michelle, Scott, Adam, Traci, Nikki, me

The lady who started it all.
My mom Nikki

Smiles all around with George.
Nikki, Traci, me, Michelle, George

**A girl's night out.
Traci, me, Michelle**

My design idea for a Spring collection.
Photo credit: Dove Shore

My design idea for a Holiday collection.
Photo credit: Dove Shore

A chic photo shot for my Babakul look book.
Photo credit: Dove Shore

Some of my original designs for True Religion.

A good partnership.
DJ, me

Eight

VISION

We were still living in Manhattan Beach when I went to file for divorce. It was not for the obvious problems in our business partnership; it was the build-up in our personal lives. But again, after some thought and a reminder of our intended mission to stay together all our lives, just before I got the paperwork written up, we reconciled and decided to move back to Malibu and try again.

Having grown up in Malibu, I still loved the peacefulness of constantly crashing waves, pelicans flying in their perfect "V" formation along the shoreline, and the expansive sky that hovers over the ocean as far as the eye can see and then connects with the water at the farthest point. Water has always been my solace, my breath, and my security.

One day while house hunting, I turned into a sloped, redbrick drive leading down to a circular car park. Beyond that, an enchanting courtyard entrance beckoned. It already felt like home. There was a basketball court along the side as we entered—the boys would like that feature.

I missed Malibu. It is a coveted enclave hiding the lucky ones, the creative ones, the bohemians, the surfers, the celebrities, and the monied, all intermingled along a world-renowned stretch of coastline.

I described what I wanted to my friend and realtor, Gayle, and she said, "There's an interesting house available that you might like."

It was a modern-inspired Mediterranean single story with a massive patio, large lawn, a guesthouse, and what ultimately became a deck overlooking the ocean. It was replete with a lap pool and Jacuzzi. There was breathing space for me, for the boys, for what was to come.

The house and yard had good bones; nine million dollars' worth of bones. And yet, I could imagine the changes I would want to make in order to make it mine. Although I was in the throes of work, I was ready to include yet another distraction. I always have several projects at any given time, most of them I'd like done yesterday, but with all that was happening with Jeff, it would make for a good change to recreate ourselves in a new house.

I thought of how Jeff would react to my desire to purchase this expensive house. As a woman, I felt my voice was not as important as his when it came to decision-making, both at home and at our company. I didn't want the same type of relationship my mom had with George, who, although I had loved him dearly, fostered an inequality in their relationship. She was a stay-at-home mom and wife until he left her in her fifties. She went back to school to become a psychologist later in life. But as we grew up, she had less say in what George brought home. He would buy a forty-thousand-dollar bronze pig on a whim, art pieces that he liked, and other expensive items for the house, with no consultation whatsoever.

I had started playing a similar role in my marriage with Jeff. But now, I wanted the freedom to have my own autonomy in my decision-making. I knew immediately I wanted the house in Malibu, whereas Jeff had other ideas.

There was a swarm of interested buyers. After exploring every inch of the property with Gayle, I said, "I love it, but I can't afford this house!"

For me, having struggled financially in the past and then to become wealthy, I still always have that unsettled feeling of being financially insecure. It is like someone who is fat and loses all the weight but still sees the heavy girl when she looks in the mirror. That is me with money. I still see the struggling girl.

However, that fear of not having money has often initiated the drive I've needed to get things done. So there is a part of me that appreciates that it is still part of my psyche.

It's a new situation for sure when you make large sums of money, especially if it is sudden. Someone has to teach you to manage your money. It's not like you get twenty million dollars and you know how to use it. It's about easing into that life and not living above your means when you get there. Treat your money like you would a business.

Don't let just anyone manage it; find someone you can trust who is qualified, unlike Billy Joel, who let his brother-in-law manage his money and lost it all. Depending on the amount you have in the bank, you may be able to live off the interest and not the principal. It becomes less of a focus when you treat it like a business. As such, you should sign all of your checks and question the charge if you're not comfortable with the amount.

I feel better knowing what I have in the bank and living off that amount. I sit with my bookkeeper every Friday and look at my P&L (profit and loss) and monthly bills. I know on every Friday what my monthly nut is. I have to manage it because it will go.

Past struggles can be helpful in pushing you today

It was a pivotal moment when Gayle assured me that we could actually afford the house. I just couldn't wrap my mind around it. The idea it could be ours at the price we offered—it was unfathomable to me. I called my best friend of thirty years, Leslie Rubin, for moral support, and she drove over from the valley that day. She'd been through everything in my life. When she saw the house, she asked, "When are we moving in?"

I had to act quickly, as there were already a lot of offers on the house. Everyone was vying for position with the realtor, desperate to have their bid be the one to get accepted.

The realtor gave Jeff, the boys, and I the house for the weekend to stay in. There wasn't any furniture, but we brought sleeping bags and slept over like we were camping out. My heart was set on this house, whereas Jeff was interested in a house in Serra Retreat, which I felt wasn't kid-conducive. He ultimately ended up at that house in Serra Retreat, but not with me.

After I put in my offer, Gayle called with a tone in her voice that concerned me. I immediately assumed it was to tell me someone else's offer had been accepted; I wasn't going to get my dream house.

"Their realtor said he'd give you the house if you give him a year's supply of True Religion jeans." That was easy!

The house went into escrow, and when it closed, we paid all cash.

The house meant so much more to me than what was on the surface. I knew being able to wake up here and in this community would bring me peace. The universe had conspired to make this work in my favor, and I was eminently grateful.

No matter what you go through, a support of a community is imperative. Having people you can count on can change your being.

Being in Malibu and knowing the city felt really good to me. I wanted my kids away from the bigger city, with all of the extra noise that can easily be a diversion from coming home for dinner or just going to the beach together. I knew it was a great way of life out here.

Truth be told, I wasn't surprised by how it unfolded with the sale. Intrinsically, I knew I was meant to live in this house. When I was seventeen, I was driving down Pacific Coast Highway with Traci and Michelle. I pointed at that exact plot of land, and I'd called it, "I want a house right there. I want to live in that spot."

Back then, there was no gate, zen garden, or rose-drenched courtyard. It was only a dirt lot that sat poised on the cliff, overlooking the ocean. Twenty-five years later, I found myself back at that same lot. It has remained my home to this day. Some things are meant to be in life, and this house was definitely a testament to miracles.

Proclaim goals, no matter how impossible they may seem

Throughout my life I have set many goals for myself, both personally and in business, big and small, long term and in the moment. But often, they become daunting. When that happens, I set shorter-term goals of something easily achievable and build on it, leading to the bigger goal. It has worked for me.

The House That Kym Built

So here I was, all these years later, feeling proud of the fact I had the opportunity to buy my dream house. Now, I was going to start trying to heal my marriage and get re-inspired with work. I had no idea about the hailstorm of shit that what was about to come next.

I was ready to figure out a solution in what my new role would be within the company, and it all felt very civil. I was totally ready to play ball and make a smooth transition into something else. What, I wasn't sure.

I did know I needed to be strategic in how I negotiated a new opportunity for myself. This was my company that I was voluntarily handing over to Jeff and the Board. I wanted to make sure I could walk out with my head held high and wanted to protect myself by creating an opportunity that would make me happy moving forward. These were savvy businessmen at the end of the day, and I wanted to make sure they were respectful of my contributions. There was a lot to think about.

It was Valentine's Day 2007. I was feeling anything but romantic. I was in my bathroom, condemning my reflection in the mirror. Stress is an amazing thing—when I am emotionally haggard, my looks are harmoniously in sync.

Jeff and I had been having a tug of war in the business, at home, with the kids, and what we wanted for our future. It was hitting a fever pitch. I had suggested he move out and buy the other house nearby us in Malibu. We were living separately with the intent that we would try this new approach to see if it would ease our frustrations with each other at work, and hopefully, soothe some of the problems in our relationship.

I should have been trying on a negligee and planning to seduce my husband, but with all the battling going on with Jeff and I, and trying to figure out how to be strategic in my move in the company, there was much to scrutinize that morning. The idea of even wearing a negligee for Jeff at that point was laughable; we barely spoke to each other. My normally ocean-blue eyes were painfully red. And my wrinkles, which were nonexistent normally, were like crevasses of war paint down my face.

I heard the phone ring, and my housekeeper buzzed someone in through the front gate entrance. A few minutes later, she beckoned me to come to the front door, where a messenger stood holding a legal-sized envelope instructing me to sign. I was not expecting any contracts, so I was a little wary at what was inside. Plus, the messenger must have needed my personal signature, since my longtime housekeeper could have easily signed for it. But as I had been practicing lately, I pushed the little voice in me aside and signed my life away. The messenger tried to stick his head inside to do a more significant scan of the interior, giving a nod.

"Nice! Let me know if you ever need a house sitter."

I was preoccupied signing his registry and wondering what I had just signed for, not to mention he was not the first stranger to have made that offer.

I could feel my hands start to shake for some reason before I had even pulled out the paperwork. Once the document was fully revealed, I gasped. There on the first page were the words: PETITION FOR DISSOLUTION OF MARRIAGE.

Jeff was divorcing me.

"Are you fucking kidding me?!" I spewed. "You motherfucker, all of a sudden you remember Valentine's Day! How perfectly ironic, you prick!"

Jeff had rarely cared about or even remembered Valentine's Day. And yet, this year, he felt the need to use it as a punctuation.

We had been married seventeen years; that's a bit of time in my book. With that many years under our belt, we had ridden the waves of happy and sad times together, had an ebb and flow of a working marriage. This was most definitely an ebb for us.

Women should marry someone who is at least, if not just the slightest bit more, in love with her, only because we go through so many changes: fat, thin, pregnant, not, hormonal, and PMS. Through it all, if he is in love with you, he doesn't see it to be as horrible as you do.

Jeff and I had gone through three pregnancies and the birth and death of more than a few companies, and through it all we had been able to maintain a steady equilibrium in our relationship. Over the last couple of years it was combative, and we were at an excruciating impasse now. But the one thing I never doubted was that Jeff and I loved each other.

We had been having discussions that maybe I shouldn't work at the company. Maybe it would be better if I focused on our boys and our marriage and walk away from the business. My biggest issue, both at the company and with Jeff, was that I felt, in being a woman, that my voice seemed less important in the last few years. Every day I found myself "shouting" louder, but felt less heard. Being that I am not exactly a silent bystander, the idea that I was feeling that way indicated there were definitely problems that needed to be addressed. I just had no idea they would be projected on a proverbial loud speaker before the world.

After I flipped through the sterile pages of the divorce petition, I feebly tried to dial my mom's number. Finally, on my third try, she picked up and I cried, "MOOOOOOOOM!!!"

In hearing the news, she told me to hold on, she'd be right there. I hung up with a sense of relief that I can only get when my mom is going to come and take care of me.

Don't underestimate the power of a hug

As much as I tried to maintain an air that I could handle everything on my own, this was a moment when I knew I couldn't do it alone. I wanted and needed my sisters and my mom like I had not in so long.

No matter how much or how little my mom had been present in my life's journey, there were pivotal moments when I really needed her, and she showed up for me. It was in those moments I was so grateful I had her there. And even if she couldn't fix it, her hug alone would give me the strength to deal with whatever came on my own. For me, it was my mom who ultimately gave me the strength to succeed, but for many people this can be any nurturing figure or mentor found in life.

St. Valentine Would Roll In His Grave

My phone rang and I grabbed it, thinking mom was calling to let me know something about her imminent arrival, so I was taken aback when I heard instead, "Hi, Kym?" I almost hung up.

Had I known it wasn't my mom, I would *not* have picked up. Now was not the time to talk with a stranger. I was annoyed at the caller, at myself, and the conversation that I would need to have in order to end the call as quickly as possible. As I started to gather my excuses, she continued, "I'm calling from the human resources department at True Religion . . ."

My mind went racing. Someone calling in for a reference? Did she need me to sign off on hiring someone? That had never been the case in the past. I was the vice president of the company and one of the major shareholders; I never dealt with human resources. But my mind was not fully functioning in that moment.

I listened in awe as she nervously explained that she was instructed to call and inform me that I had been locked out of the company and would not be able to enter the premises until the return of the board of directors in two weeks' time. My brain functions suddenly became crystal clear and I screamed, "WHAT?"

Those motherfuckers had it all calculated. And Jeff had schemed it! In order for the board of directors to know when to lock me out of the company, there had to be discussions amongst them. Here, Jeff had wooed me in to a false sense of security with, "I'm going to live over here for a while, Kym, let's see how it goes."

And at work, things were getting worked out to figure out my next move within the company—or so I thought.

I had just spoken with one of the board members the day before in a cordial conversation about his plans; the executives were leaving for two weeks to attend the Magic Market Week.

"During the time we're away," he cajoled, "take your time and pack your things, and think about what exactly you want to do next."

We had moved to the overstuffed dark brown leather chairs in his office to discuss more in depth how I was one of the biggest shareholders. His big concern was to make sure we figured out a solution that made sense for everyone.

"We are a public company, after all, and no one wants the shares to drop," he said.

He was smooth. Telling me it would be an easy transition. Everyone was in support of my decision. I was in total agreement and shook his hand as he left. It was all bullshit. He just wanted to lull me into believing all was normal until they left. And I bought into it—which is what pissed me off most.

They knew the moment my divorce papers had been signed for, which is what they needed in order to move on to their next step. That benign call I watched the messenger make as he sauntered away from my door was to the board. They were waiting for the call so that they could trigger ousting me out of the company.

I could feel the rage building inside of me. Locking me out of the company meant that everyone knew about this ahead of time. Everyone knew what was going down except me. I was devastated.

Although I could imagine that they were no doubt worried at the damage I could do during the time they were away (trust me, I was seriously contemplating in that moment what I could do to them), I hadn't considered doing any harm until that underhanded move. True Religion was my creation, after all; it would have been like harming my own child. Even in my anger, it was them personally I would have wanted to injure, not the company. Most significantly, to have my husband throw me under the bus, so mercilessly and publicly, was inexcusable.

I grabbed for my Blackberry phone to send Jeff a vitriolic email. But when I tried to scroll through my contacts, I realized my company Blackberry was disconnected. I was no longer getting emails, nor could I send any.

My rage turned to panic. My head felt as though it could burst from all the swirling thoughts. I recalled the conversations I had throughout the past few days with individuals and colleagues who knew it was coming; each memory of our discussion came with a new perspective. It was an uncanny feeling of betrayal and insecurity in every facet of my life.

Everything stopped, literally stopped, being as I knew it to be thirty minutes prior to the messenger. My mind went to my design table at my office, where I was working on the latest draft of a woman's tank and was supposed to have a fitting. Had they canceled the fitting without my knowing? I wondered what they had said to the model. Had they told her I was ejected? I had personal emails on my computer in my office. I had all kinds of projects going on. It was my office, my private space, and they had just yanked it all away from me.

I could barely breathe as I began to really harness the enormity of the idea that I was divorcing my husband and my company on the same day. And suddenly, I had this irrational fear that I had no money.

Nine

UNRAVELING AT THE SEAMS

With my Blackberry shut down, I didn't have any phone numbers, so I had to call human resources from my house phone and demand that they get one of the directors to call me at home. It was excruciating, waiting there for him to call me at his will. I was fuming. It was all so calculated.

When the very same board member who sat me in his office on that last Friday called me at the house, I screamed, "What the fuck? I left willingly, I said okay to all your requests. Then you treat me like shit! Like a piece of dirt! You get me in that office. I will sue you one by one, and I will sue all of you. Heads will fucking roll!"

I couldn't wait to get off the phone so I could start some real damage.

The Big Fight

I'm not good at being a chump, or punked, but that is exactly how I felt. The stabs in my back were deep.

I had to claw and fight and hire attorneys in order to get access to the office and retrieve my things. It took two days of intense phone conversations. It was painfully embarrassing and I couldn't believe this was happening.

Days later, on March 15, 2007, on Jeff's birthday, True Religion announced:

"Kymberly Gold Lubell, Vice President of designer jeans and casual clothing maker True Religion Apparel Inc., and wife of the company's founder, is leaving to pursue personal interests. Kym joined the company in January 2004 and worked closely in product design with Jeffrey Lubell, who is True Religion's chairman of the board and chief executive officer."

The news of it was picked up by *Women's Wear Daily*, Yahoo, and various other sites. Even though I knew they wrote the release so as not to worry stockholders, being dismissed as the wife of Jeff rather than co-creator was yet again infuriating. Not to mention the fact that they included my home address and how much I was getting paid off. So wherever it was reposted on the internet, my address was included. I called Michael Buckley in operations, but no one over there cared; they didn't give a shit. The promises that I could leave with dignity were completely forgotten.

By that point, I had retained Sharon as my divorce attorney and hired Lori, a well-known labor attorney. For the next few months, it almost became comical as I traveled from one lawyer's office to the other, about a half a mile apart in Century City. Sharon had brought on forensic accountants, family law attorneys, and a whole slew of other specialized attorneys because it was True Religion, and it felt like a lot of money. Jeff was making it difficult. He would say things like, "I'm going to make sure they find out things about you." I didn't have anything to hide, but I had no control if he made up things. It could put my custody of the kids at risk.

Jeff was so angry, accusing me of having affairs and telling the kids about it. He just wanted to hurt me through the kids. Certain things that were between he and I, Jeff would discuss with the boys. Our relationship spanned twenty years; people do what they do. He was no angel, either. I felt strongly there was no reason to drag these young boys into the divorce.

No matter how bad it is, this too shall pass

When I was going through the divorce, my mom said there was a rule. "Never open mail on a Friday. Attorneys know you can't get them on the weekend." Every time I would open the mail on a Friday, it would be a certified letter and list a negotiable point I wouldn't be getting in the divorce or something that would make my life miserable. I have not opened mail on a Friday since. Literally, never.

Jeff didn't want the marriage to end. Even with all we put each other through, neither one of us wanted that. But when Jeff got a girlfriend who was thirty years younger, it changed the dynamic.

There were also more lengthy talks with lawyer Sharon. "As your attorney I think you should fight," she said, "as your friend I can see how you could want to walk away." I wanted out so badly.

The most difficult decision in my life was in that moment, to settle for less than I am worth. There was perhaps another twenty-five million more on the table. Or I could have fought to hold on to stock. But I didn't have any more fight. I just broke. I couldn't go into another meeting. I was going to lose it. And the stress of that took me to a weight that was really unhealthy. Stress made me lose weight. I was a good fifteen pounds under a healthy weight and looked anorexic. I'm not one to not eat, but the stress took care of those calories.

I'm sure I came across like a hater, or a disgruntled woman. But I *was* disgruntled. When someone does something like that to you, you have the right to feel disappointed, and disappointed was what I felt. Between forensic accountants and labor attorneys, there was a significant staff of salivating attorneys who were trying to tell me how much I should get and how badly they wanted to get it for me.

I had debates with myself. The idea that I was getting a house paid in full and tax-free money—should that be enough? Should I stay and fight for at least another ten million? I might get it. But that fight would be ugly and long. In the end, it was not about the money for me; it was about getting my life back. I knew I could live off the settlement money. What pulled at me was that I wanted my relationship with my kids back. It had been such a scary and difficult time as I was consumed by the divorce of both Jeff and the company, rather than focusing on my boys. I wanted to get out of the daily dark cloud that I was in and see the sunshine. Once I focused on the end goal, the deal was easier to make.

I look back at that; I even talk to Sharon from time to time about it. Should I have put up more of a fight? And her answer is, "You will make that money back. Your life is not about only making the money, so I think you made the right decision."

If you're a one-hit wonder, fuck yeah, you wait for the money. If you can sell an idea to a shark tank and you have ten more good ideas behind you, it's easier to walk away.

The fact that all the other companies were mine before True Religion meant that I knew I was the brains behind the operation. I could build another company.

The moment I knew I could walk away was when I was watching a video about Africa, where these people had no water and lived on nothing. And I considered what I was paying my attorneys and where my life was at and it hit me like a ton of bricks that I was done.

I went to my attorneys, who were still vested in ferreting out every last dollar they could for me, and said, "Stop. If I wanted to stay fighting, I would have stayed married."

I had decided to be done with the whole thing and be financially liquid.

A global settlement is a very antiquated way to go. It's basically: here's your money, that's it, there's no more. There's no child support or alimony. Whatever is needed to pay out for the kids is split in half. It's a clean getaway. It was tax-free money that Jeff and True Religion had to pay out to me. Jeff had to sell shares to pay me off.

Fight . . . or choose to stop fighting

The sale catapulted me into being one of the top one-percent of earners in the world. I feel compelled to acknowledge that I am a woman who has hit that milestone. There are not that many of us.

I don't think anyone needs to be a one-percenter to be a milestone. For me, looking back, it was what I had created that no one could take away. I worked really hard and created something that wasn't just pop culture. It was like climbing the Himalayas in the snow backwards both ways. That's how I felt a lot of the time. It's nice to be reimbursed. I've always been told that hard work never goes unnoticed, and this was the culmination of that.

I agreed to thirty thousand dollars a month as a consulting fee for two years, which precluded me from doing work for any other clothing line. I found it insightful that Jeff and the board continually "assured me" that my contributions to the company were not important, and yet they were adamant they didn't want me to start another clothing line.

A New Space

I sold my shares of the company and purchased a twenty-six-hundred-square-foot loft in Venice. It was the first piece of property I had ever purchased outright without consulting one other person. I knew I wanted to work, but not at home. The loft provided a work/live space as well as a property that I could leave to my boys, a place to live after college perhaps. I liked Venice; it allowed me to celebrate that I was an artist again. It was also a close drive to home, so meetings there would be easy to coordinate. The office gave me a space where my future could unfold. Working out of my house in Malibu at the time wasn't feasible—it was far for any business venture I wanted to start, and Venice was geographically desirable. Going back to Venice had significance because I had started out on the boardwalk.

My first idea was: jewelry. When I was doing accessories for True Religion, I began to appreciate why people purchased their jewelry and what they chose. Even when an economy is down, people still buy jewelry.

In starting, I worked with a friend, Joseph Bortoli, whom I've known since high school. He made the buttons, rivets, and studs for us at True Religion when we did a limited edition. He and I worked together to create the molds and we took it to Label Tex downtown, where they mass-produced the hardware for the jeans.

Hardware on a jean is the most important part of the design. The detail of the pant is so important; it sets it apart from all the others.

Set your intention then take a leap of faith

So, although Joseph had his own store on Abbott Kinney, he came and worked for me in Venice, teaching me how to make jewelry. I created a women's line of jewelry under the company name of Babakul (which means "hippie" in French). I'd already had a company called Hippie Jeans when we worked for Paul Guez, so Babakul was sort of a cool linguistic step up.

I got reps and into stores; we were off to a good start. We got into Fragments, a high-end jewelry showroom in Soho in New York. But I couldn't compete with the people who were already on the market. Jewelry is a business of strong relationships and cliques. A lot of buyers didn't want to buy into something new; their dollars were allocated to jewelers they had been with and done well with already.

I wasn't disheartened; I yearned to design clothes again. The jewelry felt like a placeholder; I couldn't wait to get back to my true love—fashion. Money does not stop passion. But I was forewarned there would be consequences if I started to design clothes again.

I would have to stop taking the consulting fee from True Religion. It was a large chunk of money to walk away from, and it would be hard to be released of my golden handcuffs. But ultimately, I was not getting the same satisfaction from jewelry that I got from clothes.

Plus, Jeff wanted to make me miserable, and it was beginning to work.

He had become incredibly difficult. It was still a tug of war, and I was still trapped in a web with him and True Religion. Every month he would make my consulting check an issue. At the same time, I was planning bar mitzvahs for the kids with him. It was confusing, and we were not getting along.

He would do things like call his attorney to say I was being mean to his girlfriend, because I asked her to un-friend our young boys from her Facebook page (as I felt they shouldn't be on Facebook at that age). He would turn off the phone at his house so I couldn't get a hold of the boys and make me wait at the electric gate when I went to pick them up.

It was mindboggling but I couldn't cut him off—we had boys to raise. However, I *could* abolish ties with True Religion.

A Case of Amnesia

Jeff's girlfriend was becoming a pain in my ass. She was a bathing suit model and my boys—ranging in ages of eleven, fourteen, and fifteen—were hanging out with her and her friends. She was closer in age to my oldest son than to Jeff. The thought had crossed my mind several times that she may have been attracted to Jeff for other reasons than love, at least initially. I know Jeff; he's not an easy guy.

She would be ever present. At the time, I didn't think she was engaged in a way that was enhancing my kids' lives, like when I found her revealing commercial comp card in my kids backpack. And she would sit reading a *People* magazine at my kid's soccer game. It ratcheted up my concerns as a mother. None of it was sitting well with me, and I voiced it like a mother lion.

A few months prior to his dating his future baby mama, Jeff had come to me. He wanted to get back together. Some time had gone by since the divorce, so anger and bitterness had been replaced with ambivalence. I felt completely detached from him. And he wanted to rekindle what we had long ago. They say time heals all wounds; in my case, it gave me amnesia as well.

He came to me, as if he were proposing. He held out a Rolex watch box and said, "Let's have another baby. I want my family back."

In Jeff's world, babies always were the answer. The watch was beautiful, a steel strap with a pink face. He knew what I liked, that's for sure. He wanted to go on a family

Don't straddle the fence for long

trip. I do love travel, but I had gone too far forward to go backwards. That would have been cowardice.

There was a part of me that wanted to take the easy road and say yes to Jeff's request to get back together. I felt guilty that I was the one who had initiated his move out of the house and felt responsible for ruining our family unit. So questions and thoughts ran through my mind in an ongoing conversation. It would have been so much easier to go back.

"Are you sure you don't want to come back, are you sure?" He would ask many times while we were in our abyss of a relationship.

I wasn't.

The Rolex was the last real moment of indecision. The most difficult part is making the decision. I understand people get back together; I think it's normal that people go back and forth when they've been together a long period of time.

There was a fire in Malibu when I was with the kids. He arrived at the house with only his Rolls Royce. He was taking the kids to a hotel; I was going to my loft in Santa Monica. We were together at 6:00 a.m., trying to get the kids breakfast and organize their things. He said, "Why don't you just come."

It was a definite moment where we could have reconnected, but I said, "I have the dogs."

I'd known him since I was fifteen, we married when I was twenty-three, and we had shared a life together. But now, at forty-two, what I thought was acceptable behavior, acceptable sex, acceptable for me, had matured, and I knew

I did not want to return back to who I was before. As much as it was tempting to take the easy road, I knew there was the possibility we would end up separating again, and I had already gone through disconnecting our lives. I decided my new path would bring me, and ultimately our boys, more happiness in the end.

Ultimately, I finished our last conversation about getting back together with, "I'll take the watch, thank you."

When you make a definitive decision, the universe can support you. Being on the fence for any length of time is surely the most painful place to live. Of course one should debate big choices in life—make a pro and con column if that works—but long-term straddling of doing something or not can paralyze you.

Certainly, I questioned my final decision. Was I right? Would I be able to recreate the same amount of success alone that we had? Would I ever find another man to love? And would I find another man to love me just a little more? Am I too strong? Too business-oriented? Too old? Too set in my ways? The list went on and on. But in the darkest moments, there was an intuitive light present inside me that quieted my mind. In my solitude, I knew it was right to try something different. I would go out on my own. And I was going to design clothes again.

Ten

A SADDLE STITCH

It was time for me to jump off the fence and when I did, it was into my own yard. In business, I always feel like a gigantic tractor that is plowing a huge field, and there are all these things going on in the periphery as I till the soil. But, as that tractor, I continue to go in one straight line to get to my destination—detours are not allowed. As a tractor, you must move slow and steady, at times even laboriously, to keep jostling along down the field to the destination. The detours are the bullshit that comes with the work: the haters and the minutia of life.

I keep going on my path through it all.

The reality is, sometimes when I've arrived at that other side, I wasn't even aware that I had made it! I didn't even celebrate, or congratulate myself, because I was so in the moment and concentrated on pushing forward in wanting to accomplish more.

Stay focused on your destination

Babakul

In 2008, I expanded Babakul's interest into apparel. It made sense to me to continue using the name. I liked that name. I liked what it stood for, how it sounded, and that it embraced the idea of disheveled, bohemian, sexy clothing.

I wanted to do something out of the box. Having worked in denim all those years, I wanted to introduce other areas I had wanted to design: silk prints, knits, dresses, shirts, and jackets. To follow in denim as I'd already done would have been an easier way to go, but that doesn't suit my personality.

I was driven—some would say desperate—to have Babakul prove that I really was a designer, a businesswoman, and a coveted brand, so that I wouldn't have to continue to defend my importance in my last company. I could say it all day long that I created True Religion, that I was there, and that it was me with the vision. By doing Babakul, I could run away from those voices, outside and within, by creating another brand that would vindicate me. And this time the company would be mine. People and peers would know that I could create, that I was here, talented, and a force to be reckoned with in the industry.

I had longstanding relationships with Neiman's, Nordstrom's, and other specialty stores after working with them to buy True Religion and my previous clothing brands. When I started selling, buyers would complain that it was a new brand. It wasn't—it has always been me, just with a new name.

In buying my product, people could be confident that I could deliver on time and provide a good product. I'd been dealing with buyers for years with True Religion, but here I was again, knocking on doors like a beggar with a new company. That familiar feeling of being invisible was rearing its ugly head. And I didn't like it.

It's like when the leader of a popular band goes solo. Here is the band's leader, the front man whose voice has attracted listeners for years who is simply doing a solo album, and yet there's so much politics that goes into getting on the radio stations or getting a proper deal.

It was a frustrating feeling. As if all the years were a moot point.

I started going back to the trade shows. People I had hired at True Religion ignored me.

It became painfully obvious that I was being ostracized from my peers. Mickey Sills, a mutual friend, was not allowed to talk to me. Zihad, who was there from the beginning, had to sneak a hello to me. My old design assistant feared for her job after she hugged me at a show.

I walked up to Michael Buckley, the COO of True Religion, and pointedly asked, "Why are people not able to buy my line? You better tell your CEO to stop telling people not to buy my line."

It may not have been that, but that's what it felt like it was.

I wanted to make a splash for the brand, so I called Mindy Grossman, the CEO of the Home Shopping Network. I requested a meeting with her and her team. I told them who I was, and that I wanted to do a line of Babakul and sell it on HSN. They agreed. I made a sportswear line incorporating blazers, twills, knits, and jeans. From the moment I stood on their stage explaining the intricacies of the fabrics, the colors, the styles, and the fit, as the models paraded the clothes, I was astounded as the number, of pieces available for sale went down to zero.

After selling out my Babakul line, I had a better idea of how to expand their designer reach. I wanted to do a joint venture with HSN, so I organized another meeting with Mindy. This time I took her and all the executives to the top floor of the Gasenvoort Hotel in New York and stood before them as they imbibed in champagne and pitched, "Let me bring other designers to you. Let me manage bringing their product to HSN." I was music to their ears.

HSN has very high standards. They have a bible of regulations that designers have to adhere to, and their margins of profit are smaller, but the amounts sold are so big it makes it worth it.

Keep in mind, if they order from you and you don't have the goods right—the tagging is wrong, or the shipping is late—they can charge you back. That can be incredibly expensive if you have manufactured the type of numbers you need to satisfy HSN viewers. And if you don't know what you're doing with the large sizes, that too is a whole different animal, as their size scale is bigger and you need to work out how many of each size in order to sell out so you can make the most profit. When working on smaller margins, you've got to be really careful.

I called people I knew would be interested in this arena and introduced them to the buyers at HSN. Then I would either organize the manufacturing of the designers' garments and include my fee in the cost of manufacturing, or get a referral fee for the introduction and they would handle the manufacturing themselves. If it was a celebrity I brought to the table, HSN and their agent would negotiate the fee for them and I would work out my own fee depending on how long the celebrity would be on air, how many garments they sold, etc.

Independent designers I brought to HSN sold out. The executives were thrilled. However, my idea being the liaison quickly became a full-time job.

I was enjoying the fast pace of the HSN lifestyle. It suited me. It was an escape from Los Angeles. But in order for me to continue, I would have to keep traveling to Tampa on a biweekly basis without my kids. It was time to return to my base in Los Angeles. After six months, I stepped away from HSN. It was good while it lasted, but I needed to refocus my attention on being a fulltime mom.

I needed that boost at the time. I was dressing a demographic I wasn't familiar with, and I was on television doing it. I was able to see how to design fashion for less, as I couldn't offer the same fabrics I had for my higher end clothing.

It was a really great challenge for me, and I accomplished it. Talking with people while on the air was fun. Being able to dress a larger-sized woman with a stylish outfit felt good. But getting on air at 3:00 a.m. was grueling and was not sustainable for me. HSN was willing to try to do my timeframe, give me a slot the week the boys weren't with me, but I was done. It was just a choice. It was time that I get my own company on track.

Look for joint venture opportunities

I went back to my idea of making Babakul Contemporary into what I hoped would be my next True Religion phenomenon, which kept me closer to home.

I feel like I am always running with the ball. And although it's a team sport, oftentimes I feel very alone, and it is certainly not without consequences. But that doesn't stop me from liking that I have control of the ball.

If you are a CEO, head of a business, or in whatever way in charge, then be in the game and aim for the ball. What you should ask yourself when starting your own business is: Is this worth it to me? The long hours? The need to be away from my family? If it's not, don't do it. There are a lot of sacrifices to having your own company. However, if you have that "Fuck it, I'm doing it anyway" gene, you'll be in good shape. Don't go half-assed though; go both feet in or don't go in at all. Think big or don't get out of bed . . . unless there's someone big next to you.

Eleven

INVERTED HEM

People were loving Babakul, and we were gaining traction. We were at a show in Vegas, and the store Anthropologie gave us a great order. The brand was doing well in specialty stores. Those consumers enjoyed the soft knits and cargos I was creating. I felt a sense of security. Perhaps a false one.

For someone who is a smart, seasoned businesswoman, I knew better than to introduce a new brand of clothing when consumer buying was retracted, and it wasn't getting any better out there. In fact, it was getting worse. People were scared, and although there is something to be said for emotional shopping, there just wasn't the same disposable income to shop within that price point. I was more optimistic than I should have been because I didn't let that deter me. I'm not one to stop moving forward out of fear. I needed to make this work. My idea was to get my wholesale line of clothing into the stores that had been successful with selling True Religion. These people had made millions off that brand, and I felt strongly that they would know my reputation and be excited at having my next evolution.

I went to Fred Segal with Babakul. They were an immediate "Yes," and the clothes started selling really well there. I had this trouser that was the complete antithesis of what people knew me to do. Buyers knew me from denim, so from their tunnel vision, their only perspective was that I could do denim. But Babakul was incorporating styles and ideas I had in my Bella Dahl days. It was difficult to break through, as I was now doing silks and knits.

I did a whole line with vests and blazers. It was so great. No one was doing it yet; it was so cool to wear blazers and trousers. It was something at that point I thought would do well. It went into Ron Herman and other top-tier places and did well, but as is my pattern, it was ahead of its time.

Celebrities were photographed wearing Babakul: The Kardashians, Jessica Alba, Reese Witherspoon, Jennifer Lopez, Jennifer Garner, Robin Wright. There were so many who would either come to the store or have their stylist pick it up. That was always a good sign for business.

But the buyers of the major retailers kept asking why I wasn't designing denim.

Denim was saturated, and I thought it was going to be easier to go in with this new fashion-forward line. Some buyers came around. But buyers have strict guidelines and space they can buy for, so for them to buy something really new is taking a chance.

It is much easier to conform than to be at the forefront of fashion. Years later, customers at Fred Segal, family, and friends would beg me to bring back the trouser line. I should have stuck with the trousers, but I was experimenting with where Babakul was going. I wanted to know what was next. I didn't have time to sit around and wait.

No one ever wants to be first to invest in a new brand or product, especially in the middle of a financial crisis. People want to wait for that tested sure thing before they put skin in the game. By then, the designer's company has either wasted away or, hopefully, found another way to succeed.

Fashion is cyclical, and if you, a store owner, really feel strongly about a new style that is not familiar, it may take longer to get customers interested in the clothes. But wouldn't you rather be known as someone who bought something fresh and new, rather than buying something that is part of the pack?

Conversely, if you, a designer, are doing a trouser line, you may have to bring it back for a few seasons. It may take a little while to catch on. In advertising, it's subliminal. When you see a shoe and it's in every fashion magazine, suddenly people are wearing them.

Helmut Lang or Missoni do prints and zigzags that scream their name. You know when it's a Burberry. It's staying true to the branding and how you want the design. It makes you a cohesive brand rather than schizophrenic. It's important to maintain your presence until you get to a tipping point where they recognize you.

In my experience, I have found most people don't know what the hell they're talking about. That's the truth. So, in really knowing my product, and really believing in it, I have always had to become a stronger saleswoman and sell the shit out of it so I can find that other way in. I'm the one who designed it; I know every part of that garment.

Your superior doesn't necessarily know anything more than you

Designers or arty types shouldn't necessarily do sales, but no one is going to sell better than the creator. The salespeople will never know the brand as well as the designer. The salespeople who can sell a brand as well as the designer are far and few between.

Building Babakul

I ran into Molly. She had worked in production for several clothing companies, and we had run into each other at various times in our career. Originally, I was not a huge fan of her. I thought she was a real ball-buster. I didn't think she was fond of me either, so it was mutual.

She had been invited to an event at my house. We had both gone through plenty throughout the years, and in meeting again, our resistance to each other was assuaged as we got up to speed with each other's lives. When she first saw me, she called out in her gravelly Eartha Kitt voice, "Kym Lubell!"

I turned and gave her a hug, then corrected her. "It's only Gold now."

She gave a throaty laugh at that, getting the inference of my nasty divorce.

Molly and I sat together and talked more. I told her about Babakul, and by the end of the evening I had asked her to come on board.

We would go to New York and escape from our lives, go eat at Cipriani's, and laugh until we cried. We were on this journey creating Babakul together and enjoyed making the company. I knew she would have my back. She was a tough cookie and wouldn't take shit from people. She's got an edge, but I was okay with that.

I was working harder than I'd ever worked before. I had to have continuous conversations with buyers and friends about why I was designing and taking on this new line. Although the conversations were couched in clothing, it was really about my personal life. It was a taxing process to have that constant explanation for people. Then there was an expectation when the clothes came in. If it didn't fit perfectly, or the order didn't come in on time, it was heightened, and the conversation would immediately go back to the divorce and the collection and why not denim.

We had been doing well through 2008, with strong sales, especially with Anthropologie and Neiman Marcus. I had two hundred fifty retail stores that I had clothes in. During that economy, that was a good number of stores, considering it was a new business and brand. My business was factored, meaning the bank flows the money while manufacturing, and that percentage that the bank charges is built into the price of the clothes. It's such a small amount that it's fine and doesn't cut into the profits.

Generally designers pay for everything up front: the sales reps, trade shows, fabric, sewers, employees, and insurance. Everything is up front. Even the sales rep's rent is paid, and then they get their twelve to fifteen percent commission. I find that to be a bit of a racket.

The Crash

And then it hit . . . the full brunt of the economic collapse.

Suddenly it was as though the tap was turned off. I had started a company in "an economic downturn," as the politicians liked to deem it. And coming from my True Religion background, I was probably overly optimistic in what I wanted to accomplish. My Plan A was all-wholesale business to Anthropologie, Nordstrom, Saks, and Neiman's. But everyone was hurting.

The economy was killing the specialty stores—quite a few stores that carried my clothes closed, including those in Chicago and New York. My good friends' stores that I thought were invincible started closing such as Lisa Kline on Robertson Avenue, top-tier stores from Santa Barbara. It was devastating to see all these retailers I had done business with my whole career go under. The financial collapse had hit the retail industry *hard*.

As a result, Neiman's and Saks rejected my next season. It had a few more emotional layers on the cake for me, as I had paid for many a shareholder's mortgage over the years with the success of True Religion for these stores, and now I had to stand there in discussion with all new buyers telling me *No*, with my internal voice screaming *Why the fuck not?!*

It's typical for department stores to have turnover; it's a tumultuous business. If the buyer for the store buys a season and it doesn't do well, they get rid of her. The buyers who stay buy the same thing year after year to stay safe. When you're a new designer, if you do get in, they put your clothes on a small rack where no one can see it, so a week later it's—not surprisingly—on sale.

Use "No" as fuel for your tank

Sometimes I have found that buyers who say "No" are the people who want to be designers but weren't brave enough to try. I use the haters as fuel. I try to use any negativity that people give me to fuel my tank. I'll think, *Now I've got more gas. Good!*

It doesn't work every day. Some days it's, *Fuck, I hate this shit.*

Winning

Whether you have millions of dollars or nothing in the bank, there are no free passes. My initial plan to do a wholesale business was taking longer and even slid backwards with all the stores closing and losing accounts. It was a pivotal moment as to whether we would be able to sustain in the marketplace or not. If the decision was to keep going, which is generally my nature in business, then we needed to take a different course of action. Stores weren't buying from us, but I believed in our product.

Whatever it is—the loony bin gene, the Type A personality gene—whatever it is that makes us want to constantly create some new company, further some new idea, or figure out some new solution, the gene of an entrepreneur can never retire.

I just know I would like to stay at where one percent of the world lives, and my genes have taken me there, so I embrace that aspect of my makeup.

It was time for me to navigate how to be more in control of my own destiny. I just couldn't meet with Nordstrom again, to hear, "No, we're not buying what you're selling anymore. We're not looking for those brands."

I needed to figure out how to make money without paying astronomical prices for the traditional route of going to a trade show, or sitting with some young eighteen-year-old buyer for a department store, as happened in one case, who dismissively gave a whine of, "I don't really like it," while she gazed instead at the new bracelet from Tiffany's that her New York boyfriend sent over. All I could think was, "She's not even going to be working here next season, why am I wasting my time with her?"

Here was a girl in the fashion industry who didn't know who I was, about my business past, why they should be buying from me, my integrity, my business acumen, and that I deliver on time. And, in hearing my name, didn't think to do any kind of research. Hell, she could have just Googled me! Not to do so was just lazy.

My biggest pet peeve is people who don't pay their dues. Pay your dues! In my opinion there is no rhyme or reason why we have the Kardashians, who are creating crap on television and haven't paid their dues to do so. It is not okay. Oh, I'm sorry, maybe I should go and make a sex tape? I look pretty fabulous at forty-seven. I could be the inspiration for women my age, making sex tapes, and call it "Cougars of Malibu." Then maybe I'll sell more clothes?

Instead of going the "Cougars of Malibu" route, by 2010 I had found a more traditional path forward. I decided to do more e-commerce, outsourcing, and was thinking of opening my own store. It was an expensive proposition, but would allow me to surpass waiting in line for buyers. It would be a leap of faith.

I hired employees who were able to cross over into a myriad of departments. It was a do or die situation, and since it was my vision, I felt compelled to step up and take on the rest. I schlepped, I merchandised, I did whatever needed to be done. It was just like being back in the early days of True Religion, in making sure the line was cohesive, that fabrics were perfect, that they were exclusive to us. I was driving to the stores and making sure they looked perfect. All my staff needed to know customer service. Every detail was as important as the next to create an atmosphere where customers, wholesale or retail, would want to reorder.

There is honor in paying your dues

When you are spending your own money, no one is going to take care of your business as well as you. Your vision is your vision. It is oftentimes overwhelming to feel as though you have it all falling on you. The key is finding the right team.

I had brought Molly on board and had hired other talented people. And finally I wasn't feeling as though I had to toe the line completely on my own. I was ready and finally emotionally able to give my all to making Babakul work.

It's important for the visionary to be active on all fronts of the business and be hands on. If employees are doing quality work, giving them space to prove they care and are talented will be good for my business.

I don't have employees work long hours, but smart hours. If they get their work done, and do it with care and strive for excellence, I don't need them to sit at their desks for extended periods of time to make me feel good. I would so much rather have employees enthusiastic about doing the job well, and feeling as though they accomplished something. Then, they can get out of there and have a life. Smart hours, that's what I like.

But, if employees are guilty of not doing conscientious work, I have no time or energy for that type of person on my team. This is different when an employee tries a new, big idea and it fails—I still applaud that effort. When my employees bring me an idea that might be a bigger or a better idea? Fantastic! If I can implement it, utilize it, or be a champion for it, game on.

Like your friends, one should scout employees whose energy is incredibly enthusiastic, motivated, and who want to be an integral part of your success. The best CEOs never act like they know it all. They pay for employees who know what they don't know and are enthusiastic about doing it. And I can tell when someone is not. When you ask off-the-cuff questions about the line, or ask them to contribute in a meeting about their perspective, and there's not a lot of feedback. You know.

Twelve

THE COLLECTION

It was December 2010 when we had a massive grand opening in our flagship store inside Fred Segal–Santa Monica. The excitement of my first store having come to fruition was palpable. I had been contemplating how I could make a splash with a new store and thinking about the best way to get an advertising and marketing campaign started for it, when I saw Bob and Cortney Novogratz on Bravo, decorating someone's home. They were interesting to me with their two sets of twins, making them a family of seven. I really liked them on their show and they had good taste.

I reached out to them to see if they would be interested in talking about creating my Babakul flagship store at Fred Segal. Bob emailed me the next day. They were in Bali at their house. He wrote, "Absolutely interested in this. We will come back and meet with you."

They were just switching over to HGTV to do their new show, *Home By Novogratz*. I would be their first retail job, so it was going to be a win/win for all of us. From a business standpoint, it couldn't have worked out better. Because the design and build out was filmed for the Novogratz's show on HGTV, it was free publicity! There was nothing better than TV, especially if it was a popular show, to help expand my audience.

I had very specific ideas on how I wanted the store to feel. I knew I wanted the space to be homey and inviting, with one-of-a-kind floating shelves and all-natural woods that gave a flavor of driftwood, bringing in my love of the ocean. Bob and Cortney captured my intricate "must haves," and found the perfect balance of luxury and comfort in the store.

In our conversations, I explained that I wanted the Babakul logo highlighted in some unique way in the store that would capture people's attention and impress the brand on them, something memorable. They brought over miniature light boxes. Each light box hung separately and illumed an individual logo letter, with the Babakul flower emblem at the end. Against the store's brick wall, Babakul had a pronounced glow from across the room. It was a definitively recognizable stamp on the store.

My own store meant that I had more power over my destiny. My cost to retail would be much higher, so I would make a much better profit per item. I would be able to merchandise my clothing in a way that really showcased my brand, rather than hoping for some retail store to push my line.

I could decide whom I hired, how my clothes were made and presented, and how I wanted to merchandise them. And rather than have them stuck behind the cash register at a major department store, I would rather have the opportunity to handle my clothes with the care they deserved.

Later that year, a store became available in Malibu at the Cross Creek Mall. It was nestled in the back amidst James

Perse and Planet Blue, beside the new location of Mr. Chow. It offered the perfect space to introduce Babakul to Malibu shoppers, of which there were plenty.

I found my third and fourth Babakul locations almost at the same time. One in the trendy upscale outdoor shopping center called Fashion Island in Newport Beach, near the ocean in southern California. The other near the infamous Ivy Restaurant, on the equally well-known Robertson Boulevard, a coveted stretch of road where fine designers mingle with trendy boutiques, making for a little slice of shopping heaven.

Each time I opened a store, I got better at cutting costs while keeping the look and feel of the store the same Babakul quality. One of the deals I put into place with the landlords of both Malibu and Fashion Island is that they would make a set percentage of Babakul's gross sales on a monthly basis in lieu of rent for the first two years, and then once I'd been established, I would pay our negotiated rental amount starting in our third year of business. The idea with that kind of deal is that by the third year, you will be doing well enough that you can afford whatever that set monthly rent would be until the end of the lease.

I had important guidelines I wanted followed at each Babakul store: The manager and sales staff had to be totally knowledgeable about all the merchandise and the brand. They were required to wear Babakul. They must keep the store immaculate, something I was insistent on. They needed to create an atmosphere of warmth toward the customers—I wanted Babakul to have a grassroots effect, with each customer wanting to organically tell two friends about it. They would be self-initiators, to continuously think of ways to better the store, the market, and the customer satisfaction.

Many new storeowners hire their family and friends to help start up the business. Never hire out-of-work family members and BFFs when you are starting up a company. Your history becomes an issue. Their personal crises become yours. They will apologize, saying something "happened" when they couldn't make it in on time. The immediate assumption would be they had something or someone big next to them in bed . . . that's what "happened."

Quality work will be noticed

It was a huge problem for me that customer service was now underrated. I strove for excellence in the store's atmosphere of beauty and delightful sales associates. There were some high-end boutiques in Malibu where the sales associates wouldn't even greet you when you walked in. If you dropped a black card or platinum card, then suddenly, it would be, "Hi, how are you?" That was not what I wanted at Babakul. I was old school and had demanded a strong store ethic in the True Religion stores I opened in the US, and I intended on continuing that sensibility with Babakul.

It doesn't matter what profession you are in; aim for real service for customer service. "Hello" should be the bare minimum. Find out what the customer wants and what she needs, and you may have a loyal customer for life. *Is she buying something for a special occasion? Looking for a particular style?* Take time to help customers find what they need. Offer up accessories or services to go with it, get their name during the transaction, and overall just make them feel special.

I wanted each customer who entered the store to feel as though they were over at a good friend's trying on clothes. Handwritten letters were sent out, on actual paper, with envelope and stamp to thank them for the purchase. It wasn't some generic email or pre-printed postcard grossly asking, "When will you be back to buy more?" We sent beautiful notes of gratitude. We also made calls to customers to let them know of a sale on a piece they liked, or a style that had come in that they might be interested in. This all created a personal relationship between our sales team (and brand) with our customer.

My concept for Babakul was that it would not be just a store, but a destination, where customers get something back. I grow vegetables, fruit, and roses in my garden, and would handpick them to place in the store. If a customer wanted an organic apple, there was an inviting bowl of them at the counter. A go-to place, that's what I wanted for Babakul. Where people felt special and cared for, and in that relationship had the opportunity to buy beautiful, well crafted, one-of-a-kind clothes that fit them perfectly.

> **Random acts of kindness are keys to success**

I know I am particularly organized, some would even say OCD. I just like order and work better with harmonious, uniformed surroundings. If that is OCD, so be it. In either case, I look at it as a positive quality.

Working with Women

I was dismayed at seeing applicants for our various positions who had no sense of organization, or any idea how to interview for a job. Girls would constantly walk in late for the interview. As a litigator, my father taught me the sign of respect is to show up ten minutes early to a meeting, but not too early, because then it would show too much eagerness. I am always early. No matter who it is I am meeting, from my gardener to my attorney. And I will always call if I'm going to be late. So, for a young girl to walk in to an interview to work at Babakul and immediately start giving excuses, there's no reason to continue the conversation. Thank you, and next. If they couldn't make an interview on time, I could only imagine the issues that would come up if I hired them.

If I'm paying, I expect my employees' full focus on the business—not spending time texting their friends, answering their emails, and scrolling through their Instagram, which is often the case when entering many retail stores. I want their full energy on their job. Otherwise, there is someone else who could do it.

I found myself intrigued that in spending time among an all-female staff, how often the girls continually apologized for things. I would often hear, "I'm sorry I didn't enter that correctly" or "I'm sorry I forgot to say that." I'm sorry, I'm sorry, I'm sorry. What were they so sorry about?!

The only time a girl should have to say that is in a conversation with some guy, "I'm sorry, are you looking at my boobs again?" That's the only apology needed.

Having an entire company of women, I felt compelled to mentor anyone who reached out. I was always trying to instill in all the girls a strong business savvy, because I think beauty and brains should cohabitate more—they should not just be "roommates," they should be "one."

You can do *anything*, don't cheapen yourself to get a "yes"

It is important for women to know that they should be treated equally. There is a way to be a strong woman with a voice in the workplace without using sexuality, or having to yell to get a point across.

There has always been a different dynamic at Babakul because I run it differently, but in general girls need to walk into the business world knowing that there is a boys' club still going strong. They have to know it is going to be a little tougher, so they may have to work harder. Going in with that mindset, they kind of have to strap on some balls.

As a female having grown up in the garment industry, I knew men were going to call me a bitch. I just knew it. I didn't take offense. I didn't take it personally. I just stayed true to my standards. *No* was not an option. I was a "bitch" all the way, but I ultimately got what I wanted.

Along the way, I had been witness to men who tried to get away with sexualizing the relationship with their female associates, or at least testing out the water to see if the girl would let them go there. I always told the girl to hold her ground: Be sexy, be whatever you want, but never use your femininity to lure a business transaction. I took pride in the fact that I was an effective cock-blocker throughout the years.

I met lascivious guys who were working with young, cute designers who were green in the business, wanting to take advantage of them. It would happen all the time.

I know of a well-known jeans company that moved their associate designer to creative director because of an inner office relationship with the owner. There was also a popular T-shirt company where the receptionist was having an affair with the CEO. She became the top salesperson in the show room and acquired all the top accounts.

I also know of a clothing company still in business today where half the people in the company are now fashion designers because of their sexual favors. There are many companies where that happens. If that's what a girl wants to do, it's her prerogative. I believe girls should want to do it the old-fashioned way and work for it. People don't want to put in the work, but that's what makes a strong brand—putting in the work.

I'm not here to judge women for the decisions they make in the fashion industry, but if you do use sex, it affects others in the company and creates a dissension in the ranks. If it doesn't work out, then you've left yourself with nothing, and it's such a small business that you're setting yourself up with a situation that may happen again. Set up your boundaries in the beginning.

The relationships I've made along the way have been fostered in an appropriate way, with honesty, hard work, and integrity. It has affected the way those individuals I've met along the way have wanted to work with me now and in the future.

Thirteen

BRANDED

If frivolous with money, the company will suffer. Stylists were asking for free clothes to give to their clients. My first course of action was to fire my PR firm. They wanted clothes for wanna-be celebrities, and I didn't agree with that idea.

If the talent was going to wear it out and announce, "Hey, I'm wearing Babakul." Great! But the clothes were oftentimes not getting to the celebrity. So what was the point?

The money small companies have to spend giving away product in the hopes that it *might* be seen on a celebrity seems a very backwards scenario to me. I'd rather let them pay for it.

I remember one time my PR firm was in contact with the Kardashians' stylist and asked me to give them five thousand dollars worth of clothing from Babakul. Although I was against it, I gave it to them—and it never got photographed, never even got a thank you. Now, with all the celebrities having their own lines of clothing, it is also a concern that they may knock off your designs. So, in general, giving free clothes is a sticky situation. It can turn out to be a waste of money and product. Ultimately, my PR company and I had a difference of opinion, and we parted ways.

I Am My Own PR

Don't be afraid to part ways with people

I debated my decision to leave the PR company because it was true—even wanna-be reality show talent had an influence these days. It could be helpful, I knew that—I had done it successfully before with True Religion.

But times had changed. I had already given away five thousand dollars' worth of clothes at the whim of my PR agent, which didn't include their fee, and nothing had come of it. For that much money to be spent on a regular basis with no result, I believed I could do a better job myself.

I became our PR department. I reached out to editors I had known, initiated having parties, sent mail outs, and went out to social events, soccer games, or even the grocery store, wearing Babakul. We moved the money that had been allocated for PR into other areas that were more productive.

The proof was going to be whether women wanted to buy the clothes and wear them. That was what I wanted to promote. It was a slow-moving grassroots campaign, and I was intent on it getting traction.

Fourteen

TWISTED SEAMS

I let out a sigh of relief as I signed the paperwork to sell the loft I used as my office. The sale would give me a cushion to continue paying my employees, the dedicated people who had put their lives into the company for over four years. I felt as much responsibility for their welfare as I did making sure the business was a success.

Although I had intended on letting the boys use the loft after they finished college, I knew we could cross that bridge when we got there.

It had become an ongoing conversation of how much more money the company would need to stay afloat. Another hundred thousand dollars? Another twenty thousand dollars? I had arrived at a point where I was no longer giving any more of my personal money to the business. The business would have to become independent of my personal bank account.

In fashion, clothes are designed a year in advance, so I was designing a line for spring of the next year that I would be showing to buyers in September; then, jump to present day, when I was shipping for fall delivery in August while making sure that the holiday line was fitting properly. Then, I would kick into gear in my personal life to make sure the boys had the records needed for college and Dylan for high school, organize the house issues, and tend to my own personal needs. Then, it was back to work mode to review lease agreements for the upcoming stores, all while remembering to orchestrate putting money into the various accounts to pay for it all. Within each day, I would become a time traveler.

The New Men in My Life

I would do a lot of business calls as I drove into the office downtown. It was a balancing act to make sure nothing slipped through the cracks of all that was being set up with Babakul and other ventures. To keep a handle on my busy philanthropy work, home, and family I would make lists, very long lists. It was becoming quite precarious with my personal assistant, who was unable to keep up. In all fairness, there was a lot to handle. Historically, I had not had great luck with personal assistants.

On the heels of an ABC *20/20* segment I was featured in about high net worth individuals and their staffs, including personal assistants, I found a new assistant, DJ. He had an over-amplified need to be organized and was well-versed and knowledgeable in many areas. He had been sent over from an agency and interviewed by me on *20/20*. After meeting him, I canceled the other interviews. He seamlessly entered into my world and started taking over the many responsibilities within the various business arenas I was involved in.

This was the first time I had chosen a male assistant. He was even-keeled and didn't dwell on drama. He understood boundaries and didn't get involved with my personal life or issues.

I also met another man: a good man, a generous, kind, self-assured man, Marlon. I was so focused on my business that it was as though I had blinders on. I had put the idea of falling in love again out of my mind. But sometimes, it's when you aren't looking, and least expect it, that love drops on your doorstep.

Marlon had come to my house four years prior with the singer Eric Benet, our mutual friend, when I was dating someone else. He was attracted to me then and told Eric, but saw I had a boyfriend, so never pursued me. So, when Eric told Marlon he was going to my house for a New Year's Eve party and asked if Marlon wanted to join, he declined, saying, "No, Kym is in a relationship." When Eric corrected him, saying that I wasn't any longer, Marlon didn't miss a beat. "Pick me up at nine."

I was wearing a red Celine dress that had the perfect amount of cling. We spent the whole night feeling the intensity of our unrequited attraction. Each time we tried to slip away to talk, I would be pulled away by another guest. At the end of the evening, Marlon said to me, "If you're smart, you will call me."

I had always thought of myself as intelligent, so I texted him a half hour later. We got together about a week after that.

Marlon grew up black in the Deep South, having to deal with pervasive racism, where black kids were not allowed in the pool. He joined the military early and became an elite fighter pilot who flew the lean-bodied, highly strategic attack helicopter, the Cobra. I was impressed with a man who, despite all the hurdles of his life, wanted to make a difference. He was one of the few black men to fly the Cobra. He had accomplished that.

We really complemented each other. I felt like Charlotte in *Sex in the City*, when she married Harry, the Jew. A man who was not the typical type she would go for, and yet, they fit somehow.

Marlon has a quiet reserve to him, not suffering fools gladly, and when he laughs, it radiates a room and his face becomes animated in a way that makes everyone around him smile and feel at ease.

Marlon didn't "want to be" successful; he *was* successful. He had become a working actor after the military, had raised a well-adjusted child, and had an easy relationship with his ex-wife. All those qualities, to me, were evidence of a great man.

He was not intimidated by me and my successes. Instead, he said he was fueled by me. Every time he got the job or the audition I would cheer, "That's so great for us!" This relationship was like nothing I had ever experienced before. We weren't in competition. This wasn't a race. There was no drama. This was simply about support, love, and respect for each other. It was a completely new experience for me. And, bonus, it was the best sex I had ever had.

We had become each other's cheerleaders, and we both battled through our respective industries, his in entertainment and mine in fashion. But there was a renewed vigor in having Marlon in my life, championing me on.

The Golden Boys

The best part was my boys were getting on famously with Marlon, which filled my heart with joy. It made me really want to strive at building our relationship differently. I liked this newfound adult relationship.

Marlon has a great philosophy. He says, "It takes four seasons to get to know someone. You see how they are on Christmas, their birthday, and your birthday. You see how they are with family and on the various holidays. It takes the four seasons to see it all." So, quite naturally, almost at the end of our first four seasons together, we started thinking about cohabitating.

Meanwhile, Jeff and I were still clashing on our ideas of how to handle money with the kids. My theory was I would buy them a car, but they'd pay for gas and insurance. With Jake, I bought a Toyota, where Jeff bought Ryan a BMW. I understood from his perspective that he was proud he could do that for his son. He showed his love with money, but I showed mine differently. It was not good, or bad, it was just different.

Ryan and Jake were doing well in college, and Dylan was a football quarterback in high school. Jeff wanted to hand over money to the boys for a business once they got their degrees, whereas I thought there was a huge sense of personal accomplishment if they did it on their own. You couldn't teach that, they had to do it. Jeff had promised a hundred and fifty thousand to get them up and running. I wouldn't do that. Would I help? Absolutely! And the money would be a loan.

The way I saw it, just because I had money didn't mean the kids should have it. I worked for it, they should work for it, too. That was tough love for me as much as for them. I wanted to give them everything, but the importance of feeling accomplished when creating your own business is one thing I couldn't give. It was my responsibility as a parent to love and to teach them.

They are my biggest accomplishments. I have always told them that; they know it. We rarely leave a room without saying, "I love you."

It is every mother's nightmare that they are not giving enough to their children. There is no real book. There was no real anything that prepared me for a lifelong journey with my children. My constant, "I love you, I love you, I love you," followed by their, "You're suffocating me, mom." And me continuing with, "So what, get used to it." It had been the best medicine for them growing up.

Through the years, I learned I didn't have to be perfect for the boys, I just had to be there. Present. In seeing that my kids were growing up to be pretty well adjusted, I was finally beginning to feel less guilt in that arena, too.

To have control in a business sense was essential for me, but letting go of the control in my relationship and at home had now become imperative. There was so much going on with the stores and the business that it was challenging for me not to want to continue to dominate at home simply because I walked through the door. I'm sure that has been true for a lot of strong women. A woman in business has to maintain complete governance over her own company; it is a different set of rules than a man. But at home with

Marlon and my boys, I needed to have a more democratic existence.

As a woman, it feels like we're more scrutinized because we have so many other things to do while maintaining our business or career. When we're at work, of course we're worried about the kids. All those concerns go through our minds: Did they eat? Are they happy? It's a natural thought process. Men may do that, too, but it's different. For a man, it's quite the opposite. Men have tunnel vision and can focus solely on the task at hand, whereas women are multitaskers. It's usually the woman who has to drop anything and everything to handle issues with the children. It's a juggling act for us.

But my boys move me. They really take note of what I've accomplished. They see that I've opened up four stores and created this esteemed clothing company. They have a lot of respect for that and want a woman who works, who is self-sufficient. It is important to them. They all say they want someone like their mom, which means I've done my job correctly.

One day Jake said to me, "Everything you've done, you've led by example. By dating who you want, doing exactly what it is you want, doing what you say."

To hear him tell me that gave me such a sense of pride.

I can finally say it is okay to feel deserving of all of this. Marlon has given me that. My kids have given me that. They say all the time, "I'm so proud of you, mom." I feel a sense of bashful pride when I overhear their friends saying, "Dude, that's your mom?!" I like that my boys' friends are in awe of me. Being a strong woman, handling both business and motherhood, is the best thing I've done.

Fifteen

FASHION GONE ROGUE

Having more "brain space" available to me, I started to think about the big picture. I was pushing on all fronts with Babakul, but now found time to dream again, and give energy to other opportunities.

I partnered with my good friend and celebrated gynecologist in Santa Monica, Dr. Sherry Ross, who was looking into creating a chewable women's daily vitamin pack called Defy. It included a round, chewable multivitamin and a soluble omega-3. With my investment, we were able to take it to trials.

I was also approached to do a television show, something I had not considered doing, but felt could be an interesting direction. I had not enjoyed it as a younger girl, but now, having been an accomplished businesswoman, there was a different respect I was able to achieve in meetings, and having something to say now as an adult, I felt more confident and easy about being on camera. I had been on *HSN* as well as several shows, and even went through the motions of starting the show "Housewives of Malibu," which never got off the ground. Not to mention, with Babakul, I was interviewed for various magazine articles.

I like to use football analogies about success . . . No one goes after the person who doesn't have the ball. So get the ball and fucking run! Go for that touchdown!

To get to another goal line or higher level for Babakul, it meant opening up yet another store. We were not getting traction, so we decided to be in control of our sales. Cost to retail was better if we had a store. It was a leap of faith, but we'd done well with Fred Segal, and it was a great way to have editorial parties and move merchandise.

With every new store, it would add another level of stress, especially since I had made a decision to stop paying for it all out of my own pocket.

Through the years Molly and I had become close friends. We did everything together. We talked first thing in the morning, and throughout each day; we went to Cabo together; I took her to the Bahamas; we shared each other's clothes; we shopped together. She was a real confidant. We lived through the suffering and the excitement of our opening up four stores.

Even with the significant forward momentum the line was having, the company was still not breaking even. We were at a point in the business where we needed to be strategic in how we moved forward in our expansion and in what direction.

In the midst of this crucial time, Molly and I had a personal disagreement that grew into a full-out business crisis.

I was funding the company and trusted that Molly was running operations, and she was incredible, but balls got dropped. Her job included overseeing sales, and there were times she didn't manage it well. There was a significant point when I realized she should have been hiring new sales reps to carry our line, but she wasn't making it a priority.

She felt that it was extreme that I had everyone sign a non-disclosure agreement with arbitration clauses. I was adamant and needed her to put those systems in place—as the owner, I'd be the one at risk of being sued. I was the one with the deep pockets, who had everything to lose.

Molly also didn't feel we needed as much insurance as we carried.

She felt I was too strict about our sales team wearing Babakul, but that was important to me. To walk in and not see the girls greet people infuriated me. If they weren't merchandising properly, I looked to Molly, as she was head of operations. As the dollars were dwindling, the operations person needed to wear more hats, and there were so many areas that needed to be tended to, it was our job to ensure it was being done.

I was really pissed when I found out the sales team was not marking down what they were taking out of inventory to wear, which fucks up the inventory, so we couldn't keep track of our sales numbers. There was no real system and no paper trail. When lines of clothes weren't sold within a season, it became really problematic. It's a penny business, and everything adds up, but ultimately it's my pennies.

I brought in my own personal bookkeeper to take over the financial dealings. My business attorney and financial attorney said I needed to get the business funded by another source. I was becoming resentful because I couldn't fund the company anymore.

It got to the point where we didn't speak. Molly wouldn't answer my texts, and I wouldn't take her calls. We were both steadfast in our righteousness.

Our disagreement nudged my festering issue with Molly's lack of appreciation and disrespectful tone at times. More immediate to the situation, no employee was going to ignore me in my own business.

Furthermore, this goes back to how I learned the hard way not to hire someone you have a personal relationship with, and even once in business together, maintain a strong work boundary.

In the beginning of my opening up Babakul, I had not been micromanaging each department. Now that I was realizing there was a lack of production protocols in place and other issues that needed to be addressed, I became active in every aspect of the business. More importantly, I was not willing to have anyone undermine my importance in a company I had created, not again.

A residue of anger I'd held onto after my experience with True Religion came raging back. I hired a locksmith and had them come and change all the locks. Then I changed all the bank accounts. I was furious and not willing to reason with anyone. I felt justified in my anger and fired up at having to protect myself. The emotional barricade had gone up around me like a shield. I was ready to do to her what had been done to me. And I was going to "stand on high," as it happened.

I woke up, literally and figuratively, and realized I didn't want to be like those men who had hurt me. I cared about Molly. We had initiated a Herculean endeavor in opening four stores in a year. I did not want one disagreement to hold power over my business. So I called her.

She and I talked long and openly about where we stood with each other. And by the end of the conversation, although it was confrontational, it was also productive. I needed to remind her it was my business.

As CEO of any business, it can feel like the rock of Gibraltar is on your shoulders. With four stores, all the girls in my office, sales, home staff, and everyday responsibilities, the buck ultimately stopped with me.

It was a constant renegotiation of what it would take to run the business so that I didn't have to put any further money in. My goal was to make from three to five thousand a day in each store. We weren't there yet, but given the economy at the time, we were still getting traction.

So, we had to be resourceful. We had to figure out how to fund the company another way: we made an investor package and started talking to people and taking meetings with financiers; we had conversations about doing a private label; we looked at other ways to watch the dollars. Instead of going to a trade show to get attention, maybe we'd allocate one trade show fee to a salesperson who is on the road. We organized alternative ways to bring in more money, like clothing parties and trunk shows; we decided how much wholesale business was needed versus retail; we determined how to increase our e-commerce; and we figured out what to do about PR, which was still being led by me.

Before I sold the loft, I remember having a presentation there, and one of the sales reps seemed so disinterested that I asked, "Am I bothering you?"

As I talk to more businesswomen, I am reminded that I am not alone in my struggle. Those other women all have partners they don't like or want to deal with, financiers they have to appease in order to maintain the business. And we all have employees who depend on us to overcome those challenges.

It was up to me to rewrite the playbook on how I wanted to do business.

R.E.S.P.E.C.T.

When the Babakul employees saw *me*, the owner, get her hands dirty and do their jobs effortlessly, it made a difference. When they heard that I had sold my loft to keep their jobs and move the business downtown, my staff saw that compromise, and it meant something. Downtown was a trek for me, but to ensure there was a business, I would gladly make that drive.

I would buy lunch occasionally, and saying, "Thank you," is always a good idea. Or "I appreciate your work," "Happy Monday," or simply "Good morning." Those all go a long way. I treat each person as important as the next; they are all a piece of the puzzle. There is nothing I would not ask someone to do that I wouldn't do myself. I schlep, pick up garbage, even dog shit.

I had specific goals I wanted met. I felt each store was capable of doing fifty thousand a month. At the end of the month, I lamented to Marlon, "We only did $188,000 total."

"You're a little nutty," he chuckled. "You just opened a new store and are only twelve thousand short of your projection."

"Yes, but I had a goal," I said. Then I followed with, "I am a little nutty."

Marlon told me he had never met somebody who had such specific goals every day and wanted to see each of them come to fruition.

The truth is, I feel comforted by having goals. It gives me a gauge of whether I need to either step it up, or check it off my list. I am not good at resting on my laurels, so it becomes more about making a more extreme goal if I hit my target. And sometimes I don't hit the target.

A couple of years ago, I reached out to Mickey Drexler at J. Crew. I was impressed by Jenna Lyons, Mickey's long time designer. I thought I would like to see about doing something with her for J. Crew. Mickey said, "Hey Kym, how are you? To what do I owe this fabulous phone call?"

If you always obtain your goals easily, make loftier goals

I thought, *Wow, you want to talk to me?* There are times I still can't believe CEOs want to talk to me. And then I fluctuate to thinking, *Yeah, you better want to talk to me.* I can be a walking oxymoron.

Anyway, Mickey passed along Jenna's contact information and I left her a voicemail, but she never called back. I have no idea why she didn't return my call. But the point is, I had to at least make the call. I was nervous because you never know what will come from the other end. But it was another opportunity to put myself out there. It's not about the result, it's about the journey.

Most of the time I have to call again and again. *Neiman's hasn't called back. I have to call Bloomingdale's again.* And I get mad. *Fuck, I made you millions and you can't call me back!* Of course, they all call back when your line does really well.

On the flip side, I am appreciative of the opportunities that passively present themselves to me. I did a Babakul line for Anthropologie because they saw the store in Fashion Island, a shopping center in Newport Beach. They have a great Anthropologie there, and their buyer saw Babakul. I had been questioning whether it had been a good idea to be in Fashion Island, but that's where they saw my line.

An editor of a local Los Angeles magazine went to the Robertson store and said, "Oh my God, I love this store!" It intrigued her enough to want to do an article. I viewed her enthusiasm for the store as an advertisement. The stores were my mouthpiece.

My biggest lesson with Babakul was to know that no matter how successful you are, you must continue to wear many hats and stay connected to the business. You can never feel too rich, too smart, or too successful.

Sometimes that frame of mind can be frustrating, and I feel like I am moving backwards to prove myself. Then I talk to God, or whatever the higher power is in the universe. One night I said, "Listen, Universe, what are you doing? Have I not proven myself? Are you making it hard on me again to prove that it doesn't come that easy? Because I get it. I know it doesn't come that easy."

When I can't see the way, I will go underwater in a meditative state and ask the universe, "Please help me. Give me an answer." Sometimes I don't get the answer, but I do have a toolbox of experience to figure out the answer on my own, or the knowledge to know enough to hold off and wait. I give myself that all-too-important space of time to let things unfold naturally and let the answer come to me organically.

I can't reiterate enough how setting goals and being organized has helped me stay afloat as a businesswoman and mother. It is not about only having vision for your business, but also for your entire life! You should have a vision for how you want to look, feel, and express yourself, and then just live it! My day looks like this: I usually work from home Monday and Friday. And no matter what, I work out at least four days a week, because I know that will help in whatever else I need to do for the rest of the day. So I get that done in the morning. I know it sets the tone for me. If I'm going to the office, I make my own lunch, so I go to work knowing I'm nourishing my body with clean food. I have a protein drink before I leave. I take probiotics, and my Defy vitamins. If I don't nourish myself—mind, body, and soul—I am not at my best. I'm not here to preach or say, "Do this or that," but what I have found is that my body and brain have to work as one, because they're kind of attached and I would like them to stay that way.

I'm not gluten free, I'm not vegan, I simply eat foods that make me feel good. If it doesn't make me feel good, I won't eat it again. If I want a piece of bread periodically, I'll do that. I grow my own fruits and vegetables. I use as much as I can from there—my own avocados, three types of lettuce, mint, rosemary, basil, cucumber, potatoes, blueberries, oranges, watermelon, lemons, and limes. Those are the ingredients I have to choose from.

I live by what my acupuncturist told me, "Everything in moderation, even excess." I believe if I live up to 85 percent of how I want to eat and workout, it gives me permission to have 15 percent of cheating—just enough room to be kinder to myself.

Always be kinder to yourself

I know myself, and I am an overachiever, so rather than dwell on some slip I had with having sugar, or not working out one day, if I think of it as being an 85 percent success rate—that gives me room to grow, and room to live.

When I got divorced, it hit me—I'm on my own to live life on my terms. At almost fifty, to think like a twenty-something, like I have to wax my legs or he's not going to have sex with me because I have hair on my legs, or worry constantly whether my hair looks good or that I didn't work out hard enough. . . . I have to give myself a percentage of the best of what I can do, and then I've got to let it go.

It's the same with worrying or praying. I can either worry or pray; I can't do both. Pray I have a successful day today, or worry I won't. Worrying can get debilitating and gets me nowhere. I choose praying. It is a less anxiety-provoking mindset.

With where I live, worrying about the commute never feels right. I am lucky to have the opportunity to drive alongside the pristine California coastline to my own personal haven. If I complain about that, I'm afraid the universe will take it away.

I believe in karma, and although I was brought up Jewish, I think of myself as more spiritual than religious in a biblical sense. There are too many radical "religious" people who have turned out to be perverts or completely deceptive individuals. I have more of the belief that the universe is working in its way, whatever that is, and that there is some higher being of connection and people. That does not stop me from having conversations with God, or a higher power, or the universe, whatever you want to call it. I like those conversations and have them often.

Sixteen

A ROLLING RACK

It was right before the holidays in 2013 when Rick, my financial advisor, flew in from Austin to meet with me. His first words were, "What the fuck are you doing? You can't put any more money into the company."

It was becoming glaringly obvious I needed to get a more consistent flow of money into the business. I called Molly because it should be her problem, too. We discussed putting everything on sale for half off in each of the stores through January. Meanwhile, all my vendors were calling.

The expectation was to do four hundred thousand a month because it was Christmas. If the pieces were full price we would have made that goal, but because it was all on sale, we made half that. Now with four stores, there were taxes on each and a bigger payroll output. There was an intense need to get the company subsidized from other areas. I needed more wholesale and more private label. In order to keep everything afloat, I needed to do a good three hundred thousand a month. After liability insurance, rents, and everything that goes into running retail, that is the money it would take to keep us propped up until the stores could finance themselves.

I have never bounced a check; my word has always been my bond. The struggle for me in the situation was in having to tell people, "I can't pay you right now."

I also had to prioritize payments to my vendors, which was a painstaking task.

Did I pay the liability insurance instead of a vendor whose jewelry was doing well in my stores? Liability insurance could wait two months, as opposed to a jeweler who is an artist and someone I admired and wanted to continue to have in the store. It makes me very uncomfortable to be late; that is not how I do business.

And there would need to be a reason given as to why I could not pay someone on time. Certainly if they fucked me over, that would be a reason. An example would be one sales rep who decided she wanted to get rid of our line in the middle of the season and wanted to get paid for all the work Molly had done.

I had gone over and above to give all my reps the tools they would need to sell the line: a great product; lookbooks; my integrity; I shipped on time; we had great customer service; a flexible exchange policy; a strong social media presence; and a cool website. Even with all that, the rep and her sales associates had done nothing with the line. They had that blasé attitude that I detest. And yet they certainly became animated once they were ready to get paid. I will not, for the rest of my life, pay somebody for laziness. I'm not doing it.

I had allocated a certain amount of money to invest in the business from my True Religion buyout. With the redesign of the business structure to include the four stores,

I had put all the money in I could afford. Now, as hard as it was to face, the business would either sink or swim.

Sink or Swim Investors

There was an interesting dichotomy happening in my life. I drove to work in either a Bentley or Range Rover, yet I couldn't pay my vendors. And they all knew how I live. It didn't appear to make sense. But it was the dawn of a new day, and I had to make business decisions from a place of resolve.

Now, heading into the holiday season, I needed to take an honest evaluation at what I would have done differently in starting the company, and every step thereafter. It would almost be a waste of time unless I learned something. If I had another twenty million I wouldn't think about it, I would continue to move forward. But I had arrived at the end of my financial road and we were not yet buoyant enough to continue on without some financial assistance on my part each month. It wasn't even a lot each month, but after four years of putting in the money necessary to get it up and running, I couldn't sustain it.

Entrepreneurs need to be mindful when making up their infrastructure on a new company; don't necessarily spend money on your projections of how many pieces you can sell based on past relationships. Don't be too overly optimistic about how much you can sell out of the gate, even with your wholesale business in mind. If you decide you want to sell your goods in a store rather than waiting for wholesale orders, make sure you are mindful of costs on your flagship store. Don't let your costs get out of hand in your enthusiasm; you may need to open others or allocate that money for something else.

A flagship is usually a significant store and I did like the statement it made for us, but it was an extravagance that I would have curtailed. All my Monday morning quarterbacking was a little too little and a lot too late.

In reading through my financials with Rick, it was true—I didn't have the money anymore to allocate to the company. I didn't. Not with a property tax bill of over a hundred grand on my house. I had to get a line of credit from a bank or get some outside financial support. It was time to look at getting investors.

I paid a hefty sum to get an alluring investment book together to attract investors.

When we opened the boutiques, we had to switch all of our numbers in our business plan, which would have indicated a profit. But because of our adding on those additional retail stores, the financials had all been rejiggered to include that cost, which plummeted the numbers to show us at a loss, even though we had decent retail and wholesale numbers. But what I was working on doing in the end would make us a profit. The initial financial outlay looked high on paper.

With each step I pondered how best to attract an investor. And when I did bring one on, what kind would work best for what I wanted to accomplish? A strategic investor? A minority shareholder?

I had very specific ideas about where the company could be in the next five years. That said, I knew next month I didn't want to have to write another check. I also wanted to make sure we didn't appear desperate. We had to pick the right investment company to grow us.

In any business, no one ever wants to appear desperate. Confidence is an incredibly important attribute when you're doing anything. It's like dating—when you're trying to find a guy, you want to appear confident, then that person wants to go out with you, or in business, they want to work with you. If you're afraid of the horse, it'll buck you off.

I started meeting with investors, and their comments were all similar: the company wasn't big enough for them. But because I have the reputation, they were interested enough to want to track us.

I often had people asking why I needed an investor. I wanted to choke them. *Why?!* My kind of business is the type that investment funds and finance groups would allocate their money to invest in. I had built the foundation, and it was a perfect, and necessary, time to find other money to put into the company. A good friend's son worked over at Advent Venture Partners and recommended us to him. Advent had bought Coffee Bean and Lululemon. Clearly we were not big enough for them yet, but by having a conversation with that investor, he offered an introduction to a smaller company who dealt with companies our size, saying, "Once they can get your company big enough, that's when we'll step in."

We set up that next meeting. So often it is a relationship that is the kick-off to bringing the right persons together.

The talks with investors were difficult ones.

I learned so much from True Religion. There was a knowledge and insight into the fashion industry that I had in creating another strong brand. The various formulas I had used for True Religion—the formula for opening stores, branding, and marketing—enabled me to successfully open Babakul. But not all of it worked in the same way anymore; we were in a new time in our industry and in our culture.

The discourse with Molly got worse, and our inflamed personal relationship started overriding the business needs. I looked at my barometer and realized the difficulties were outweighing the strengths. I needed to take back control of the business, so we parted ways. Now with the entire company back on my shoulders, I had to find someone else to be the operations manager. I was so busy dealing with the day to day of the company and stores that I couldn't deal with other deals and other opportunities, which had potential to be quite lucrative.

I could have found another production manager, I could have continued searching for the right investor, but with each month that I kept the company up and running while doing so, I would be ignoring my fiscal responsibility to myself and my family. The income was still not balancing out with the expenditures. So after much consideration I decided the smart business decision, as hard as it was to make, was to close the company. It was the right thing to do.

Even though I had made that call, I still felt I had a duty to everyone involved in Babakul. For my landlords, I found another clothing store to take over each of my locations, and for my employees, I had made a deal with the incoming stores that they would re-hire my staff. The others in my office I helped to find employment elsewhere.

With my leftover inventory of clothes from the stores, I held charity events/sales parties at my home, with part of the proceeds going to a breast cancer charity and a no-kill animal shelter. The rest I handed over to an consignment company that would sell off my merchandise and pay off the rest of my debts. I felt good in getting everyone paid, settled, and working as I closed down the company.

It is not to say it was not hard. There were a myriad of emotions I felt during the process. Certainly there was the fact that I had put in a chunk of money, but it was worth every penny and every minute. It had been a great life raft when I had needed one most. The renewed confidence I gained as a designer was significant for me. And although I was closing this company, my design work was not ending, so my creative needs were going to continue to be fed. Even with the sadness, there was a sense of freedom that came with it. After getting through the endless red tape of closing Babakul, there was a lightness to my soul that was undeniable.

Seventeen

THE NEVER-ENDING RUNWAY

True Religion ousted Jeff in May of 2013. They paid him a nice golden parachute to leave. After he was gone, I had a meeting with the new executives. The idea that I was going to sit in the very offices of the company that had ejected me some years earlier in a painfully savage manner, to discuss possible future business—well, it was cathartic.

I was told by one of the board members and their interim CEO, Lynne Koplin, that they'd had no women's line once I left. They had nothing. "You are the missing link," she said.

This meeting was a vindication for me.

In our discussions at True Religion, we talked of my doing private label work for them. There was a sense of accomplishment in going back, having created my own company. It felt as though we were meeting on more equal turf. Obviously their turf was higher priced, but I had something they didn't—a designer.

Two weeks later, it was announced that True Religion was being sold for almost a billion dollars to the private equity company TowerBrook Capital Partners.

Once again, I took that opportunity to make a call. This time to TowerBrook. The partner heading the True Religion deal, Andrew Rolfe, was the former president of Gap International and chairman and CEO of Pret a Manager. TowerBrook bought and sold other luxury lines such as Jimmy Choo, and had many holdings, including the St. Louis Blues hockey franchise. It is a multi-billion-dollar investment group that buys large companies. The moment I saw it was sold, that very moment, I called Andrew.

The fact that Andrew took the call so quickly was a major coup for me.

"I'm nervous," I admitted to him on the phone. "I wanted to call and congratulate you because you just bought my baby. I've waited a long time to make this phone call. I knew something like this would happen."

He was impressed by my reaching out, and we talked about the deal and their excitement at taking over the brand. I ended the conversation with, "I'd love to have a discussion next time you come out."

He replied, "Absolutely."

When Andrew came to Los Angeles, he took a meeting with me downtown. Lynne Koplin also sat with us. Again they reiterated that I was their missing link. No one had taken over women's since I had left, they kept pulling from the archives of my designs.

I made my case that I could bring True Religion a lot of product, which would be advantageous for them because most denim companies are becoming full fashion houses. With the 25 percent tax to send denim over to Europe, it no longer makes sense to only do just jeans.

With the leather, sweaters, and knits that I have, everything that I do could be right in line with what they need. I have everything that could bring the name back to True Religion. Mine is a fully realized line.

Andrew was sincere. "You seem incredibly enthusiastic and you obviously know what you're doing. It's a pleasure meeting you. Let me go back to my office, let me think of what I need to do. I'll do my due diligence, and let's continue the conversation."

I shook his hand. "I'd like that."

He got back to me after our meeting and said that he needed to let the dust settle before he made any big decisions. Apparently there was still very much a Jeff and Kym camp presence in the company. I had been so optimistic that we could make it work that his email was a letdown.

In response, I wrote an emotional email to him. I didn't proofread or edit the email, I just wrote honestly and unfiltered. I may have stabbed myself in the foot with that one. But then again, that's who I am. Take it or leave it. I am someone who wants to fight for her company with commitment and love.

As for True Religion, in continuing to look for a yes with them, in a redemptive full circle of my life, their CEO David Conn and his team met with me to see about doing a knit line for them.

DJ and I walked into the True Religion offices, located in Vernon. Sitting in the large lobby, we watched as people ran back and forth between the women's and men's sides, abuzz with their racks in a flurry of activity. As we waited for David to join us in the lobby, DJ pointed out that none of these people in the company would have a job if not for my vision and perseverance those many years ago.

David and I had a deep discussion about what they wanted in rebranding, their interest in enticing a more committed and consistent buyer, and where they see their e-commerce going. In finding myself back in the company, being asked for my opinion on everything from store décor to what I thought of their current designs and merchandise, I felt an exhilarating thrill of pride for the success of the company I had helped to create.

When you're in business, even though emotion should not be present, passion should be. Oftentimes, women are treated as though they are overly emotional when they simply have passion for what they are doing. It's like standing up for your child. *Are you fucking kidding me? Don't touch my kid.* That's not emotional, that's love.

I had to learn to be proud of my passion, not fear it, and now I am happier than I have ever been. The last time I was this joyful was when I gave birth. There is an internal shift that has happened in my spirit, enabling me to maintain a lightness from within. A laugh or smile is now easily at the ready—and I maintain a standard of kindness toward myself. Not just any standard . . . a gold standard.

ACKNOWLEDGEMENTS

With all my love I'd to give a special thank you to . . .

My sisters, Michelle and Traci, who are my constant support and love me unconditionally.

My little brother Adam, whose wit gets me through.

My children, Jake, Ryan, and Dylan, who are my biggest accomplishments.

My rock, Marlon, who has shown me what love really is.

With gratitude, I'd like to acknowledge the following for their support and for their contributions to this book . . .

I'd like to give a special thank you to Sharon Soboil for working with me on this personal story that seemed at times very difficult to get through, and for helping me to have a sense of humor along the way.

Derick LaSalla, for encouraging me to have the strength to tell my story.

Michelle Zeitlin, as my literary representative, who believes in me and this book and is an unwavering support in getting my story out.

Krishan Trotman at Skyhorse Publishing, who has been a great partner in the process.